In Fulfillment of Their Mission

The Duties and Tasks of a Roman Catholic Priest:
An Assessment Project

Joseph Ippolito, M.A.
EDC Senior Project Director

Rev. Mark A. Latcovich, Ph.D.
Vice Rector and Academic Dean, Saint Mary Seminary
Wickliffe, Ohio
President, Midwest Association of Theological Schools

Joyce Malyn-Smith, Ed.D.
EDC Director of Strategic Initiatives in
Workforce and Human Development

National Catholic Educational Association

In Fulfillment of Their Mission

The Duties and Tasks of a Roman Catholic Priest:
An Assessment Project

A Partnership of the
Midwest Association of Theological Schools
and Education Development Center, Inc.

Supported by funds from the Wabash Center for
Teaching and Learning in Theology and Religion.

Policies for Distribution & Use of Published Materials by the NCEA

In Fulfillment of Their Mission: The Duties and Tasks of a Roman Catholic Priest is published by NCEA Seminary Department with the express permission of the Midwest Association of Theological Schools (MATS). The materials included in this monograph were developed by a MATS task force in partnership with Education Development Center Inc. (EDC). This MATS project was funded by a grant from the Wabash Center for Teaching and Learning in Theology and Religion.

The contents of this publication may not be reproduced without the express permission of the Midwest Association of Theological Schools (MATS). For assistance and questions about the use and reproduction of these materials, contact MATS President Rev. Mark Latcovich, Ph.D. at mal@dioceseofcleveland.org or the NCEA Seminary Department as indicated below. The Profile, "In Fulfillment of Their Mission" and associated "Rubrics", ©Education Development Center, 2007 are reprinted with permission. All other rights reserved. For more information or permission to reprint, use or duplicate the Profile and Rubrics please contact Joseph Ippolito at jippolito@edc.org

For information on this and other publications, projects and services of the NCEA Seminary Department, contact: Bernard F. Stratman, SM, Executive Director, Seminary Department, NCEA, Suite 100, 1077 30th Street, NW, Washington, DC 20007; Telephone: (202) 337-6232; Fax: (202) 333-6706; E-mail: seminary@ncea.org; Web: www.ncea.org

For information on the services provided by the Education Development Center, see www.edc.org or e-mail Senior Project Director, Joseph Ippolito at jippolito@edc.org

Purchasing Information

To order copies of *In Fulfillment of Their Mission*, contact:

NCEA Member Service Center, Suite 100,

1077 30th Street, NW, Washington, DC 20007

Telephone: (202) 337-6232; Fax: (202) 333-6706

Email: services@ncea.org

Web site: www.ncea.org/store/index.asp

Single & Multiple Copy Purchases

Single copies: $24.00 each. (NCEA Member discount 33%)

Multiple-Copy Pricing for NCEA Members. (S&H added to each order.)

1-5 copies: $18.00 each

6-9 copies: $16.00 each

10 or more copies: $15.00 each.

Book design: Deb Green Design, (925) 462-5023

TABLE OF CONTENTS

PROJECT OVERVIEW

Introduction

This document presents a profile of what a successful Roman Catholic pastor needs to know and be able to do. It draws primarily upon the *Program of Priestly Formation*, in particular the four pillars of priestly formation, as well as, *Pastores Dabo Vobis* and the *Basic Plan for Ongoing Formation of Priests*. It is influenced by developments in the areas of spirituality and cultural diversity. It is informed by the experiences of successful priests and seminary educators.

We hope that this document will serve as a catalyst for discussion among seminary faculty, as a framework for curriculum review, analysis of syllabi, and faculty study. The materials here may be useful in designing portfolios that assess the seminary student's intellectual and pastoral development, and may offer guidelines for shaping healthy behaviors that impact spiritual and personal development. Seminarians will gain a fuller understanding of the scope of liturgical, pastoral, and spiritual leadership as well as the necessary commitment to on-going formation. Continuing Education Directors will find the document provides potential tools for the self-assessment of individual priests and for further development of programs aimed at augmenting ministerial skills. Vocation Directors will notice that the document offers a concise picture of the pastoral duties and tasks of a priest in ministry today and may be used to help potential candidates discern their vocational call. Lay leaders will value this comprehensive ministerial portrait that illustrates the canonical and theological ramifications of presbyteral leadership as they intersect with their own shared responsibility with pastors.

Our intent has not been to create a definitive set of fixed norms of priestly duties and tasks but rather to create a helpful template for ongoing discussion. This document will need to be applied to local settings, adapted for a specific region or diocese, and integrated into a specific cultural context. We realize that no priest engaged in ministry performs all of these duties and tasks. Some are delegated to others. Nevertheless, priests from various regions in the United States and Europe have reviewed this document and affirm that the portrait presented here captures the essential nature and scope of ordained ministry today.

The profile reveals that the successful priest values solidarity with the Church's magisterial teaching, diocesan bishop and presbyterate; fosters a deep liturgical and personal spirituality; engages in ongoing theological reflection and invests energy to learn the skills required for pastoral leadership, collaboration, and delegation.

The profile has its limits. It does not provide all of the answers on how successful seminarians or priests create and implement plans for personal growth and development. However, the sample rubrics illustrate what successful ministerial performance looks like at various stages in the pre- and post-ordination formation process. This material also provides examples of how this template might serve in seminarian assessment using a portfolio model.

The faculty representatives of the
Midwest Association of Theological Schools

In Fulfillment of Their Mission

The Duties and Tasks of a Roman Catholic Priest:
An Assessment Project[1] *

Devising a strategy and creating tools to assess the development of seminarians for the M. Div. degree poses a daunting task for seminary faculties. On the one hand, the aim of theological education offers resistance to the application of formulaic assessment models that ignore "the nuanced and complex goals of theological education."[2] On the other hand, existing standardized guidelines lack sufficient detail to allow for objective appraisals of student performance. Compounding these difficulties, few faculties share best practices in assessment and have not had the opportunity to wrestle with these issues with colleagues from other theological institutions. Also, few seminaries have considered adapting assessment strategies that have proven effective in other professions as a tool to strengthen their mission of theological education.

For the better part of two decades, the Association of Theological Schools (ATS) has been at the forefront of efforts to examine and introduce current theory and best practices to the community of theological educators. Their work highlights the hesitancy on the part of faculty to embrace objective measurement because of the belief that the "outcomes of a seminary education" are best assessed through a process of "professional judgment." This judgment is often subjective and based upon experience in the field. However, there is always a need for a more precise articulation and objective measurement especially within the areas of professional development and skill acquisition in the learning taxonomies associated with ministerial training.

John Harris and Dennis Sansom suggest that professional judgment by experts can be strengthened by a greater degree of objectivity when a common language is developed for student assessment.[3] This can be achieved through ongoing dialogue among educators who share the same content knowledge and inhabit a common "language community" with their students. That shared language reveals to students what they are expected to know and be able to do. It provides for educators what they are expected to teach and how they might assess student performance.

In Fulfillment of Their Mission: The Duties and Tasks of a Roman Catholic Priest, and the scoring rubrics that accompany it, are products of an ongoing dialogue of such a language community. That dialogue has brought together academic faculty representing eight seminaries affiliated with the Midwest Association of Theological Schools (MATS) and senior staff representing Education

---

[1] The title is drawn from the USCCB Fifth Edition of The Program of Priestly Formation, 2005, section 23: "For priests, the specific arena in which their spiritual life unfolds is in their exercise of ministry in fulfillment of their mission."

* The project was funded by a two year grant from the Wabash Center for Teaching and Learning in Theology and Religion.

[2] Daniel Aleshire, *Theological Education,* Autumn, 1998.

[3] John Harris and Dennis Sansom, "Discerning Is More Than Counting", American Academy for Liberal Education, March, 2000.

Development Center, Inc. (EDC). MATS is a forty year old association of twenty-four Roman Catholic seminaries from the midwest, southwest and west coast that holds an annual meeting in Chicago to discuss issues surrounding seminary formation, administration and best practices regarding seminary programmatic development. EDC is an international, nonprofit organization that conducts and applies research to advance learning, and provides technical assistance and support to translate new knowledge into policy and sustainable practice. EDC currently manages 325 projects in 35 countries. Its Center for Education, Employment, and Community programs has more than 15 years experience developing standards-based assessment in fields ranging from manufacturing to information technology.

Through a two-year grant from the Wabash Center for Teaching and Learning in Theology and Religion, MATS and EDC have fashioned a new way for educators and students to view the full range of responsibilities of ordained priests in the Church today. *In Fulfillment of Their Mission* offers a profile of what it is that a successful priest needs to know and be able to do. It draws upon the expertise of active priests and seminary faculty members. It illustrates how widely recognized methods of occupational analysis can be adapted to address the distinctive nature of the priestly vocation. It provides a foundation upon which seminary faculties can begin to build assessment strategies and portfolios that offer objective measurement of the activities that describe ministerial performance.

There is of course a limit to how extensively a standard occupational analysis can be effectively applied to the priesthood. In the spirit of *Pastores dabo vobis*[4] and as the *Program of Priestly Formation* (PPF) asserts, "Formation, as the Church understands it, is not equivalent to a secular sense of schooling or, even less, job training."[5] Application of the occupational analysis model has been enhanced to reflect the human, spiritual, pastoral and intellectual domains of formation. This modification has not eliminated the inherent tensions between an occupational and a vocational view of the priesthood. Nevertheless, we believe that *In Fulfillment of Their Mission* represents a fresh vantage point from which Roman Catholic seminary faculties and their students can view their formational goals.

Background

Since 1971, Roman Catholic seminaries have organized themselves following the guidance of the PPF. Through the PPF, now in its fifth edition, the U.S. Conference of Catholic Bishops establishes norms that specify the curricular content of seminary education and priestly formation. Based upon these norms, seminaries help each candidate engage in vocational discernment to embrace the identity, skills, and mission of a Roman Catholic priest. What the norms do not prescribe are methods by which seminary faculties should gauge the progress that seminarians achieve along their journey to ordination. As a result, seminaries typically approach the subject of seminarian assessment in isolation. Frequently, seminary formation faculty establish their own criteria for judging student performance.

---

[4] John Paul II, Pastores dabo vobis (I Will Give You Shepherds: On the Formation of Priests in the Circumstances of the Present Day) (Vatican City: 1992). Pastores dabo vobis is a seminal document on the identity and role of the Catholic Priest in the advent of the New Millennium.

[5] Program of Priestly Formation, Fifth Edition, section 68.

This allows a seminary to shape its evaluation processes to reflect its unique institutional culture. Yet it does not provide a common basis for assessment across seminaries because of the uneven development of criteria. Moreover, this type of evaluation lends itself to a more subjective judgment of candidates.

MATS and EDC have engaged in a process that seeks to explore the possibilities of creating more objective methods of evaluating student performance. The project brings together seminary leaders in an effort to generate consensus about how best to create an infrastructure upon which authentic, objective assessment measures can be developed. It is a project driven by four interrelated questions:

- To what extent can the priestly vocation be described in language that lends itself to objective assessment?

- To what extent can a framework for assessing the ministry of a priest take into account the behavioral attributes that constitute the core of the formation process?

- To what extent can methods used to develop assessments in other professions be applied to the Roman Catholic priesthood?

- To what extent can this strategy lead to the creation of tools that are useful to seminary faculty and those responsible for the ongoing formation of priests?

Using a performance-based approach

The MATS/EDC team centered its discussions on the development of a performance-based assessment framework. This approach replicates best practices used to create training programs and authentic assessments in other professional schools. At the same time, it parallels the scope and nature of ministerial formation which often requires, as ATS notes, the dimension of time.

> The attainment of learning goals in a professional degree program like the MDiv cannot be fully determined while students are in the degree program, or even at the time of graduation. MDiv students are being educated for performance ministry, and some learning goals cannot be assessed until graduates are in ministerial settings…and the graduate is in practice in the field.[6]

Like ATS, MATS and EDC understand that it is from the vantage point of ministerial performance that seminarian learning can fully be gauged. It is the integration and application of learned skills and behaviors that constitute the portrait of successful formation. Consequently, by examining the responsibilities of a priest in the field, outcomes can be defined that optimize the quality of education in the seminary.[7]

Developing the profile of a priest in ministry

Effective assessment begins at the end. Clearly defined goals enable educators to provide substantive feedback to their students. For the purposes of developing an assessment framework for seminarians,

---

[6] ATS Handbook of Accreditation, Section Eight, "A Guide for Evaluating Theological Learning", p.7.

[7] Ibid. p.10.

this meant creating a statement that appropriately defines the end point for further deliberations, i.e. the goal of seminary formation. To do this, the work team adapted EDC's concept of a "Learning Occupation".[8] A Learning Occupation is an invented construct that does not exist in the workplace; nor does it correspond to a specific occupational title or description. Rather, it represents the combination of all tasks, knowledge, skills and attributes required to perform a range of job functions conducted in a group of related real-life occupations. The Learning Occupation construct draws on best practices in worker training in Japan and Germany, where cross-training of technical workers is considered critical to ensure high-quality work. It has been used by EDC in Industry Skill Standards projects to articulate an outcome goal for the education and training of workers whose responsibilities cut across different, related occupations.

EDC's methodology was used to create a starting point for reflection about a contemporary portrait of a Roman Catholic priest in the field. While the main mission of seminaries is to prepare men to become priests, recent studies have suggested that seminary graduates become pastors within three to five years.[9] As a result, the "Learning Occupation" that emerged was that of a Roman Catholic priest with pastoral experience rather than a recent seminary graduate. Thus the panel's proposed Learning Occupation reads:

> A Catholic Priest serving the people primarily in parishes, and also in schools, hospitals, prisons, and other settings, through acts of Christian Ministry including celebrating liturgy and sacraments, education, administration and pastoral care.

This definition of the Learning Occupation paints a limited landscape of the priesthood in so far as it takes into account only the types of ministry a priest may have and the main duties of performance by a priest. It is understood that the nature of priestly service is linked with its identity (in particular, the spiritual and theological aspects of the vocation). That is to say, priesthood is more than an occupation. Nevertheless, as a point of reference, the generic nature of this definition promotes easier articulation of the primary and secondary responsibilities of a diocesan priest, and provides clear and useful limits within which the daily work of parish priests can be described.

The definition of the Learning Occupation became the subject of a modified DACUM analysis facilitated by EDC. DACUM (Developing A CUrriculuM)[10] is a method for practitioners in an occupational field to identify the major areas of work and the constituent tasks that define successful job performance. Methods like DACUM rest upon three basic principles:

- Expert workers can describe and define their job more accurately than anyone else.

- An effective way to define a job is to describe precisely the tasks that expert workers perform.

---

[8] Judith Leff and Monika Aring, *Gateway to the Future: Skill Standards for the Bioscience Industry,* (Newton, Massachusetts: Education Development Center, Inc., 1995), 27.

[9] Dean Hoge, *Experiences of Priests Ordained Five to Nine Years,* National Catholic Education Association, Washington, D.C., 2006.

[10] Robert E. Norton, *DACUM Handbook,* (Columbus, Ohio: 1997). The DACUM process has been widely promoted by Robert E. Norton and the Center on Education and Training for Employment at Ohio State University.

- All tasks, in order to be performed correctly, demand certain knowledge, skills, resources and behaviors.

For the purposes of this project, a panel representing eight seminaries was assembled that includes seven ordained priests: all have served as parish priests, six have seminary teaching experience, four currently serve or have served as academic deans of theological schools, one is a member of a religious community and one is an ATS administrator. The panel also includes: two women religious with teaching and administrative experience, and four laymen with various levels of expertise in administration, teaching and assessment.[11]

The focus of the ensuing guided dialogue hinged upon descriptions of concrete, observable activity performed by priests. Participants were encouraged to envision a *successful priest*[12] as defined by the Learning Occupation. They described a parish priest ordained between three to five years serving as a pastor. Participants were challenged to identify *all* ministerial activities undertaken by such a priest and express them by using a single verb and object. The final wording of each activity statement was achieved through group consensus. The purpose of this exercise was to achieve a high degree of specificity and clarity in the description of activities performed by the priest. This activity facilitated the eventual development of objective assessment measures.

Once all activities had been identified by the panel, they were organized around major areas of ministerial responsibilities (i.e. duties) and their constituent tasks. This organization of responsibilities is depicted as a matrix listing the duties and tasks of a Catholic priest and can be found on pages 16 and 17. To complete this profile, the panel identified those elements that enable a priest to perform these activities. In short, these include:

- The skills and knowledge necessary for a priest to perform his responsibilities;
- The behaviors, or attributes, demonstrated by a successful priest;
- The resources necessary for a priest to perform his responsibilities successfully.

This listing does not claim to be exhaustive, but as a whole it provides a fairly complete picture of what skills, knowledge and behaviors a priest in today's Church is likely to exercise in ministry. Lastly, the panel identified major trends and concerns that define the current context in ministry and the resources necessary for its performance. These lists may be found in the appendices, beginning on page 87.

Reading the priest profile

In Fulfillment of Their Mission captures and organizes the information solicited from the MATS panel through a rigorous guided dialogue process. The matrix developed by the panel displays nine ministerial *duties* (major areas of responsibility) and their constituent *tasks*. The nine duties are listed numerically for ease of reference (and not priority) to include:

---

[11] See page 14 for a complete list of panel members.

[12] The qualitative variable successful priest is understood to mean one who has "achieved levels of ministerial performance" that meet the prescriptions of church teaching, canon law and skills that reflect pastoral sensitivity with ministry (see the appendix of prescribed rubrics).

- Celebrates Liturgy and Sacraments
- Provides Pastoral Care and Spiritual Guidance
- Teaches the Faith
- Leads Parish Administration
- Practices a Ministry of Presence with Parish Groups
- Participates in the Life of the Diocesan Church
- Engages with Diverse Publics
- Engages in Professional Development
- Engages in Personal Development

The tasks run horizontal to the duties in adjacent columns. Each task is referenced with the duty number and a letter. For example, the task "Celebrates Eucharist" is referenced as (1A) indicating that it is the first task for Duty One. Similarly, the task "Visits the sick and others in need" is referenced as (2A) to indicate that it is the first task of Duty Two, etc. The tasks have been sequenced to approximate an order of priority. The collection of duties and tasks in this Learning Occupation intends to describe as completely as possible the activities of a successful priest in ministry.

The profile serves two immediate purposes. First, it communicates to prospective seminarians precisely what will be expected of them as future priests. Secondly, it summarizes for educators what it is they need to prepare these students to know and be able to do. Faculties at several MATS seminaries have begun to review and discuss utilizing this profile in the following ways:

- a faculty retreat day to review formation priorities,
- as a guide for the recruitment of prospective candidates,
- as a framework for curriculum review,
- as the infrastructure for an MDiv portfolio that may evolve into a capstone project, and
- as a foundation for developing a post ordination growth plan for newly ordained priests.

Validating the profile

The panel that contributed to the development of *In Fulfillment of Their Mission* brings a high degree of expertise and experience about priestly ministry and preparing men for the priesthood. The consensus of the panel is that the profile provides a dependable description of the duties and tasks of priests today. Further verification of the profile's accuracy was sought from active priests in the field. EDC customized its previously developed on-line occupational survey to accommodate the specific content of the panel's work.[13]

The aim of this validation process was to produce a document that authentically represents the work of a priest and that has broad applicability. The survey asked respondents to do four things:

---

[13] The survey was developed as part of EDC's Information Technology Across Careers (ITAC) project which was funded by the National Science Foundation.

1) to provide basic demographic data about themselves and their parish,

2) to determine the importance of each identified task in the performance of their ministry,

3) to identify the frequency by which each task is performed, and

4) to review the additional lists developed for the profile (skills and knowledge; behaviors; resources; and current context).

The combination of importance and frequency scores were used to understand the "view from the field" of the priorities of ministerial work.

During the fall of 2006, the survey was piloted by making it available to a sample of active priests provided by the MATS panel. This trial run resulted in 76 completed surveys. The demographic profile of the respondents is summarized as follows:

- Average age: 51.9 years;

- 80.7% Caucasian, 7.7% Hispanic/Latino, 2.6% Asian, 1.3% African-American, 6.6% Other;

- 62% have 20 or more years experience in the ministry;

- 25.7% held a career in another field prior to becoming a priest, with the majority of these having been involved in either business/industry or education;

- 47% serve in a suburban setting, 43% urban and 11% rural.

Respondents were asked to review all duties and to rate the relative **importance** of each task by a five point Likert scale ranging from "essential, very important, important, somewhat important and not applicable". Following each task, a **frequency** measure was used with response categories ranging from "daily, weekly, monthly, rarely and not applicable" to determine how often each task was performed. In addition, each respondent had an opportunity to provide individual comments. Results from the survey show that the respondents agree that *In Fulfillment of Their Mission* provides an accurate picture of a priest's responsibilities. They also concurred that the panel's ordering of the tasks for each duty approximates the degree of importance those tasks have in the field.

Assessing the performance of a priest's duties and tasks

EDC has used occupational analyses as the basis for creating assessment tools in a variety of career fields. In the case of the helping professions, EDC has learned that effective interaction with clients typically demands that workers possess special attributes like compassion, active listening and the ability to empower individuals to make their own decisions. The degree to which these attributes exist proves to be difficult to evaluate. For example, in New Hampshire, EDC worked with Human Service professionals to contextualize such qualities in order to facilitate their assessment. Descriptive statements were created that provided examples of what the job tasks of human service workers "look like" when they integrate specific attributes. These descriptions of observable job tasks and attributes were then sequenced to illustrate levels of performance mastery. These levels became the basis for assessment.[14]

---

[14] This example is drawn from EDC's New Hampshire Skill Standards Implementation and ITAC projects.

The project panel replicated this strategy using the four domains from the PPF, and developed examples of what these domains looked like when they are performed in various tasks. These examples of performance were organized into sequences illustrating levels of proficiency.

Reading the rubrics

A rubric is a scoring tool that specifies the level of performance expected for several levels of quality. It is a set of criteria used by instructors to assess student performance. Rubrics clearly communicate degrees of proficient performance to instructors and students alike because they offer instances of achievement that are observable and specific. Building off of EDC's experience in creating rubrics for other career skills programs,[15] the project panel created rubrics for each of the nine duties described in the profile. The full set of rubrics may be found beginning on page 19.

The rubric for each duty is organized around four *performance levels* that show incremental levels of achievement. These levels range from novice, approaching proficiency, proficiency to above proficiency. By definition, the novice level represents the performance of what would generally be expected of a recent graduate from seminary. One would see the potential presence of pastoral skills that still require further development. The level designated as "approaching proficiency" indicates a more highly developed skill level and a more mature integration of the four domains of formation. The level of "proficiency" lists sample performance statements that describe a stage of skill development expected of a pastoral leader. Finally, the performance level "above proficiency" includes statements that indicate exemplary service and ministry. In many ways the minister becomes a role model and minister to his peers.

The left column on the rubric charts lists the *performance area* for the duty being analyzed. Performance areas generally coincide with the *tasks*.[16] Each performance area is broken into *performance statements*. The performance statements are used to describe levels of mastery within the performance area. Each performance statement illustrates an activity that integrates a task performed by a priest that incorporates one or more of the dimensions of formation (guided by the PPF and PDV). The numbers and letters following each performance statement signify tasks that may be assessed using that same statement. The dimensions of formation integrated into the performance statement are indicated by the *italic* letters – I (intellectual), H (human), S (spiritual) and P (pastoral). For example, under Duty One and adjacent to the performance area "Celebrates the Eucharist" the first performance statement indicating achievement at the novice level reads "Celebrates the rite accurately in its various options and rubrics". The numeric and lettered references following the statement

---

[15] EDC's ITAC project is one of several recent initiatives that have developed scoring rubrics.

[16] In some instances tasks in the profile have been combined or slightly reworded to facilitate assessment. For example, in **Duty One**, "Celebrates Liturgy and Sacraments," tasks (1D) "Celebrates Reconciliation" and (1F) "Anoints the sick," have been merged as one performance area under a new heading called "Celebrates the sacraments of healing." The panel felt that the performance statements listed were equally applicable for each of these two tasks. Similarly, the panel felt that tasks (3I) "Communicates message of faith through various media" and (3J) "Represents the Church's point of view in the public arena" could best be assessed by combining them under the performance area "Uses the media to communicate the message of faith."

denote alignment to tasks 1A, 1C, 1E and 1G indicating that each of these tasks can be measured by the same performance statement. In addition, this performance statement integrates the intellectual (I) and pastoral (P) domains required here. The collection of rubrics charts includes similar cross referencing between performance statements, tasks and dimensions of formation.

Using *In Fulfillment of Their Mission* and the rubrics

As noted on page 10, MATS seminaries and diocesan offices are beginning to reflect on various ways of applying *In Fulfillment of Their Mission* as an assessment tool. In several focus groups of seminary personnel, it was felt that the instrument can serve to benchmark faculty reflection on the various levels and components of formation. At most seminary faculty discussions intellectual formation is the focus. The profile and rubrics have provided a new approach to discuss and integrate the human, spiritual and pastoral domains into an assessment of the curriculum. Several seminaries are beginning to incorporate these tools as part of a portfolio that students and their formation and spiritual directors may use for personal goal setting and periodic review.

A few priest focus groups have felt that the profile and rubrics could become a template for individual priests to evaluate and set goals for their own growth as a minister. One director of continuing education suggested that the project can become a guide for individual priests, as they set personal goals and strategize how they might improve their ministry. Many valued the examples of performance statements found in the rubrics as they exemplify various levels of proficiency providing a way to help priests to assess themselves in a current ministerial context. A focus group of priests from the Archdiocese of St. Andrews and Edinburgh (Scotland) have reviewed these documents and noted the universal applicability it has to their own context.

A national validation of the priest profile is currently underway. EDC has revised and posted the validation survey on-line. Roman Catholic priests serving in the United States are invited to take the survey by logging onto **http://surveys.edc.org/cleveland/dacum3.htm**. Directions for completing the survey can be found at this site. EDC is currently establishing a Web site to share these and other materials and to host online dialogues about them. Those seeking information about the Web site should write to: jippolito@edc.org

Those seeking further information about these materials, or seeking technical assistance in their use can contact:

Joseph Ippolito
Jippolito@edc.org
(216) 451-1142

Reverend Mark Latcovich
mal@dioceseofcleveland.org
(440) 943-7639

Project Panel Members

Rev. Mark A. Latcovich, Ph.D.
Saint Mary Seminary and Theological School
Wickliffe, Ohio

Sr. Elaine Brothers, OSF, Ph.D.
Rev. Kenneth Hannon, OMI, Ph.D.
Oblate School of Theology
San Antonio, Texas

Terrence Callan, Ph.D.
The Athenaum of Ohio
Cincinnati, Ohio

John Gallam, Ph.D.
Sacred Heart School of Theology
Hales Corners, Wisconsin

Rev. Todd Lajiness, Ph.D.
Sacred Heart Major Seminary
Detroit, Michigan

Rev. John Lodge, S.T.D.
Christopher McAtee, D.Min.
Rev. Martin Zielinski, Ph.D.
University of St. Mary of the Lake/Mundelein Seminary
Mundelein, Illinois

Msgr. Jeremiah McCarthy, Ph.D.
Association of Theological Schools
in the United States and Canada
Pittsburgh, Pennsylvania

Sr. Karen Shirilla, SJ, Ph.D.
Saints Cyril and Methodius Seminary
Detroit, Michigan

Thomas Walters, Ph.D.
Saint Meinrad School of Theology
Saint Meinrad, Indiana.

EDC senior staff Joseph Ippolito, M.A., and Joyce Malyn-Smith, Ed.D.
designed the conceptual approach and facilitated the development process.

Thanks to Rev. Rodney Kreidler, Saint Angela Merici Parish, Fairview
Park, Ohio and Rev. Damian J. Ference, Faculty, Borromeo Seminary
Wickliffe, Ohio, for participating in the initial brainstorming session.

THE NINE MINISTERIAL DUTIES OF A CATHOLIC PRIEST

DUTIES	TASKS				
1 Celebrates Liturgy and Sacraments	**1A** Celebrates Eucharist	**1B** Preaches liturgical homilies	**1C** Initiates children and adults (Baptism, Confirmation, Eucharist)	**1D** Celebrates Reconciliation	**1E** Officiates at weddings
2 Provides Pastoral Care and Spiritual Guidance	**2A** Visits the sick and others in need	**2B** Counsels parishioners	**2C** Offers spiritual direction	**2D** Provides assistance or referrals to social/community services	**2E** Responds to crisis situations
3 Teaches the Faith	**3A** Preaches the Gospel	**3B** Evangelizes the community and culture	**3C** Models a living witness of the Gospel	**3D** Implements RCIA processes	**3E** Prepares people for sacraments
4 Leads Parish Administration	**4A** Initiates strategic planning (vision/goals/programs)	**4B** Oversees implementation of strategic plan	**4C** Participates in parish, pastoral and finance councils	**4D** Animates parish ministries, apostolates and volunteers	**4E** Oversees parish finances (e.g. budget, fundraising, diocesan assessment. . .)
5 Practices a Ministry of Presence with Parish Groups	**5A** Participates in parish groups (e.g. youth, older adults, divorced, bereaved . . .)	**5B** Greets people before and after liturgy	**5C** Attends parish functions	**5D** Acts as liaison among parish groups	**5E** Visits schools/religious education (RE) programs
6 Participates in the Life of the Diocesan Church	**6A** Cooperates with Bishop	**6B** Encourages priestly/religious vocations and lay ministry	**6C** Collaborates with presbyterate, deacons, religious and lay ecclesial ministers	**6D** Interacts with Presbyteral Council	**6E** Attends deanery/district meetings
7 Engages with Diverse Publics	**7A** Promotes community outreach, justice and peace programs (e.g. shelters/food pantries)	**7B** Builds relationships with diverse cultural groups	**7C** Mediates theologically diverse intra-ecclesial perspectives	**7D** Participates in advocacy groups (e.g. Pax Christi, pro-life, death penalty, save the children, immigration reform...)	**7E** Engages in ecumenical and interfaith dialogue and activity
8 Engages in Professional Development	**8A** Maintains a habit of theological reading and reflection	**8B** Acquires new skills for ministry	**8C** Participates in a priest support group	**8D** Consults with mentor/peers regarding pastoral practices	**8E** Engages in ministerial self-evaluation on a regular basis
9 Engages in Personal Development	**9A** Maintains a life of prayer	**9B** Receives spiritual direction on a regular basis	**9C** Participates in yearly retreat	**9D** Nurtures healthy friendships (family/friends)	**9E** Maintains health (e.g. attends to diet/exercise/ physical and mental health)

1F	1G	1H	1I	1J
Anoints the sick	Celebrates the Order of Christian Funerals (wakes/funerals/burials)	Leads devotional practices (e.g. Stations, Rosary)	Coordinates liturgical planning	Oversees the training of liturgical ministers

2F
Initiates canonical (marriage) procedures

3F	3G	3H	3I	3J	3K
Coordinates areas of faith formation (e.g. adult, youth, children)	Catechizes adults, youth, children	Responds to questions of faith	Communicates message of faith through various media	Represents the Church's point of view in the public arena	Conducts retreats

4F	4G	4H	4I	4J	4K
Oversees parish programs	Employs parish staff (hires/fires/evaluates)	Supervises maintenance of physical plant (Church, school, grounds)	Manages parish staff (supervises/supports)	Implements diocesan policies	Supervises parish communication

5F	5G
Visits families' homes/dinner	Mediates parish conflicts

6F
Supports diocesan initiatives

7F
Serves on civic, religious and community boards

8F	8G	8H
Contributes to development of the profession (e.g. writes articles, conducts research, interacts with thought leaders, gives presentations)	Develops a collaborative leadership style	Develops multicultural sensitivity

9F	9G	9H
Maintains balance and flexibility in schedule	Takes days off and yearly vacations	Manages personal finances (e.g. charitable contributions, plans for retirement . . .)

The Matrix:
Duties and Tasks
of a Catholic Priest

serving people primarily in parishes, and also in schools, hospitals, prisons, and other settings, through acts of Christian ministry including celebrating liturgy and sacraments, education, administration and pastoral care.

Rubric Key

The rubric charts that follow are organized by duties (major responsibilities) that appear in the profile of a priest (*In Fulfillment of Their Mission*). A rubric chart for each of the nine duties described in the priest profile is provided.

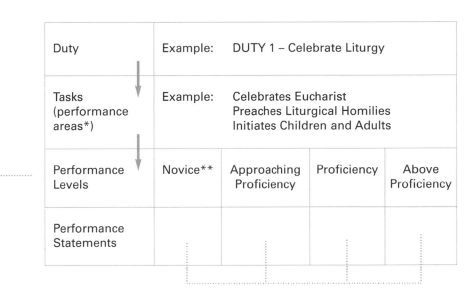

Duty	Example:	DUTY 1 – Celebrate Liturgy		
Tasks (performance areas*)	Example:	Celebrates Eucharist Preaches Liturgical Homilies Initiates Children and Adults		
Performance Levels	Novice**	Approaching Proficiency	Proficiency	Above Proficiency
Performance Statements				

Each chart includes four performance levels (novice, approaching proficiency, proficiency, above proficiency) that indicate incrementally more advanced levels of achievement. Every duty is subdivided into performance areas. The list of performance areas for a duty generally coincides with the tasks identified for that duty in the priest profile.

Each performance area is further subdivided into performance statements that illustrate activities within the performance area that integrate one or more of the dimensions of formation.

After each performance statement are references that indicate integration of tasks and domains of formation (i.e. the Pillars of Formation from the Program of Priestly Formation).

- The first bold font number and letter signify the task from the priest profile most fully integrated in the performance statement.

- Subsequent bold font numbers and letters indicate examples of other tasks from the priest profile that are integrated in the performance statement.

- Italicized bold font letters indicate domains of formation integrated in the performance statement (*I = Intellectual, H = Human, S = Spiritual, P = Pastoral*).

* In some instances, tasks taken from the Priest Profile have been combined or slightly reworded to facilitate assessment.

** The performance statements listed under the category "novice" approximate the minimal levels of what a newly ordained priest should be able to do.

Celebrates Liturgy and Sacraments

| Performance Area | Celebrates the Eucharist |

Novice

Celebrates the rite accurately in its various options and rubrics. (1A, 1C, 1E, 1G) *I/P*

Inspires the congregation to a sense of reverence for the Eucharist. (1A, 1C, 1E) *S*

Communicates the presence of God at various liturgies. (1A,1B, 1C, 1E, 1G, 1H) *S*

Articulates the words of the ritual so that the congregation understands and can participate in the Mass. (1A, 1C, 1E, 1G) *H/I*

Approaching Proficiency

Makes appropriate accommodations in time, use of language, gestures and use of space that demonstrates an awareness of the needs of the congregants. (1A, 1C, 1E, 1G, 8H) *P*

Projects a prayerful disposition in liturgies- composure, physically communicates the import of the event. (1A, 1C, 1E, 1G, 9A) *S*

Celebrates Eucharist and sacraments with appropriate affect avoiding dullness and histrionics. (1A, 1C, 1E, 1G) *H/P*

| Performance Area | Preaches Liturgical Homilies |

Novice

Prepares a homily that follows standard homiletic structure with a single focused message and thematic connection from opening to closing. (1B) *I*

Articulates clearly and uses language easily understood by diverse groups in the congregation. (1B) *H/I*

Delivers a homily that fits the context of the fullness of the liturgical act. (1B) *I/S*

Approaching Proficiency

Delivers a homily that demonstrates sound exegesis of the readings and includes an understanding of the historical context of the writing. (1B, 8A) *I*

Incorporates an understanding of the daily lives, attitudes, culture and history of the local congregation in his preaching. (1B, 5A, 5C, 8H) *S/H/I/P*

Proficiency

Celebrates the order of Mass so that the rite flows naturally and communicates solid sound theology (historically critical, doctrinally responsible, accurate to the development of the rite…). (1A, 1C, 1E, 1G, 8A) *I*

Engages the community in their duty and responsibility associated with the Eucharistic celebration. (1A, 1C, 1E, 1F) *I/S/P*

Utilizes the opportunity for evangelization in the celebration of the Eucharist. (1A, 1C, 1E, 3A, 3B) *I/P/S*

Utilizes in a generous and compelling way liturgical symbols, vesture and accoutrements for the fullness of meaning. (1A, 1C, 1E, 1G) *I/P*

Manages seamlessly the spiritual and logistical environment throughout the Eucharistic celebration. (1A, 1C, 1F, 1G) *P/S/H*

Above Proficiency

Fosters a deeper Eucharistic spirituality in the celebration of the rite. (1A, 1C, 1E, 1G) *S/I*

Comforts, inspires and challenges the congregation to carry the Eucharist to the world. (1A, 1C, 1E, 1G, 3A, 3B) *P*

Proficiency

Preaches homilies that establish connections between sound scriptural exegesis, current issues and the lives of the people in the liturgical event. (1B, 5A, 5C, 8A, 8H) *I/P*

Speaks out of an awareness of the differing convictions of listeners. (1B, 5A, 5C, 5D, 5G, 7B, 7C, 8H) *I/P*

Above Proficiency

Varies style and content of homilies in creative ways to engage the listener. (1B, 8A, 8B, 8H) *I/H/P*

Mentors others in developing their homiletic skills. (1B, 8F) *H/P*

Inspires the community to service and action. (1B, 3A, 3B, 4D, 7A) *S/H/I/P*

Celebrates Liturgy and Sacraments

Performance Area | **Initiates Children and Adults (Baptism, Confirmation, Eucharist)**

Novice	Approaching Proficiency
Celebrates the rite accurately in its various forms and rubrics. (1C) *I/P*	Uses the celebration of the RCIA to express the joy and festivity of the Easter mysteries. (1C) *P/H*
Celebrates the rites with appropriate adaptations for children and adults. (1C) *P/I*	Emphasizes the conversion process in the reception of these sacraments. (1C, 3G) *S/I*
	Celebrates the rites in a way that manifests an understanding of the RCIA process in the parish. (1C, 3D) *I/P*

Performance Area | **Celebrates the Sacraments of Healing (Reconciliation, Anointing)**

Novice	Approaching Proficiency
Displays good listening skills. (1D, 2B, 2C, 5G, 7C) *H/I*	Communicates the presence of God in these sacraments. (1D, 1F) *S*
Celebrates the sacraments according to the rubrics. (1D, 1F) *I*	Inspires the congregation to a sense of reverence for the sacrament. (1D, 1F) *S*
Displays humility and non-judgmental attitude. (1D) *S/P/H*	Aids the person in self-reflection. (1D, 2B, 2C) *S/I*
Shows empathy to the person. (1D, 2A, 2B, 2C) *I/P*	Helps the person appreciate the graces of the sacrament. (1D, 1F) *S*
Assigns appropriate and just penance. (1D) *I/P*	
Offers appropriate counsel. (1D, 2B, 2C) *H/P/S*	

Proficiency	Above Proficiency
Celebrates the sacraments of Initiation in a manner that moves the congregation into a deeper awareness of their Christian identity and responsibility. (1C, 3A, 3B) *S/P*	Engages the neophyte in the mystagogical process so as to further initiate them into the life of the parish community. (1C, 3G, 8A) *I/S*
Utilizes in a generous and compelling way the symbols of water, oil, light, garments and gestures for the fullness of meaning. (1C) *I/P*	Calls the congregation to a deeper commitment to the mystagogical process. (1C, 3G, 8A) *S/P*
Utilizes the sacraments of Initiation as an opportunity for evangelization. (1C, 3A, 3B) *I/P/S*	Helps the family of the neophyte understand the dynamics of the RCIA. (1C, 3D, 3G, 8A) *I/P*
Takes opportunities during the celebration of the RCIA liturgies to instruct, inspire and affirm the community as models and witnesses. (1C, 3A, 3B, 4D) *I/S/P*	

Proficiency	Above Proficiency
Communicates the mercy, forgiveness and healing of Christ in the reception of the sacrament. (1D, 1F) *S*	Creates a culture and an environment in the parish that promotes healing and reconciliation through the sacraments as normative and essential. (1D, 1F, 3G) *S/H/I/P*
Calls people to a deeper spiritual identity and maturity through the reception of these sacraments. (1D, 1F) *S/I*	
Comforts, inspires and challenges both the individual and the congregation to conversion and healing. (1D, 1F) *P*	
Establishes connection between the scriptures and situation of the person. (1D, 1B, 2C) *S/I*	

Celebrates Liturgy and Sacraments

Performance Area | Officiates at Weddings

Novice	Approaching Proficiency
Shows sensitivity to the family dynamics of bride and groom, and their families. (1E, 8H) *H/P*	Fosters a spirit of community for those gathered at the wedding. (1E) *P*
Celebrates the rite accurately in its various forms. (1E) *I/P*	Integrates ethnic customs into the celebration. (1E, 8B, 8H) *I/P*
Expresses the joy and festivity of the occasion. (1E) *P/H*	Establishes connections between the scriptures and the couple's life commitment. (1E) *I/P*
	Helps the couple understand their role as ministers of the sacrament. (1E) *S/P/I*

Performance Area | Celebrates Funerals

Novice	Approaching Proficiency
Celebrates the stations of the rite accurately in its various forms (wake, liturgy and committal.) (1G) *I/P*	Integrates ethnic customs into the funeral celebration. (1G, 8B, 8H) *I/P*
Shows sensitivity to the family by learning about the deceased, their history, circumstances of death, etc. (1G) *H/P*	Delivers a homily that incorporates sound exegesis of the readings and makes appropriate references to the deceased, without eulogizing. (1G, 1B, 8A) *I/P*
Communicates the comfort, mercy and forgiveness of Christ, the Good Shepherd, and His promise of eternal life. (1G, 3A) *S*	

Proficiency	Above Proficiency
Helps the couple understand the sacramentality of their commitment. (1E) *S/I*	Creates a culture and an environment in the parish that promotes sacramental marriage and family life. (1E, 3B) *S/H/I/P*
Utilizes the opportunity for evangelization in the celebration of this sacrament. (1E, 3B) *I/P/S*	
Utilizes in a generous and compelling way liturgical symbols, vesture and accoutrements for the fullness of meaning. (1E) *I/P*	
Engages the community in their duties and responsibilities in relation to marriage (e.g. modeling faithful marriages, praying for newly married couples, support for children). (1E, 3G) *I/S/P*	

Proficiency	Above Proficiency
Utilizes in a generous and compelling way liturgical symbols and gestures for communicating the meaning of the Paschal mystery. (1G) *S/H/I/P*	

DUTY ONE

Celebrates Liturgy and Sacraments

Performance Area | **Leads Devotional Practices**

Novice	Approaching Proficiency
Identifies and appreciates existing devotional practices in parish. (1H, 8H) *P/S/I*	Empowers others to lead devotional prayer in parish life. (1H, 9A) *H/P*
Offers catechesis to the parish on devotional practices. (1H, 3G) *I/P*	Integrates ethnic devotional customs into the parish life. (1H, 1A, 1C, 1E, 8H) *I/P*

Performance Area | **Coordinates Liturgical Events and Training**

Novice	Approaching Proficiency
Communicates parish protocols and diocesan guidelines for the celebration of liturgical events. (1I, 1J, 4J, 4K) *H/P*	Develops a calendar of liturgical events in conjunction with staff and committees. (1I, 8G) *I/P*
Works with people celebrating sacraments and committees to plan and organize liturgical events. (1I, 8G) *H/P*	Conducts and evaluates training sessions for liturgical ministers. (1J) *I/P*
Identifies the ethnic liturgical customs of the community. (1I, 1J, 8H) *I*	

Proficiency	**Above Proficiency**
Helps people value authentic devotional practices in relation to the liturgical and sacramental life of the Church. (1H, 2C, 3G) *S*	Discerns the use of additional devotional practices arising from the needs of the parish community. (1H, 5A, 5D, 5G, 8H) *H/P/S/I*

Proficiency	**Above Proficiency**
Offers retreats and days of recollection for parish liturgical ministers. (1J, 3K) *S/H*	Develops new protocols, practices and schedules for liturgical events as a result of assessment. (1I, 1J) *S/H/I/P*
Assesses the quality of liturgical life in the parish on the basis of liturgical documents. (1I, 1J) *I/P*	
Integrates ethnic customs into the planning of liturgical celebrations. (1I, 1J, 1A, 1C, 1E, 1G, 8H) *I/P*	

Provides Pastoral Care and Spiritual Guidance

Performance Area | Visits the Sick and Others in Need

Novice	Approaching Proficiency

Novice

Empathizes with suffering. (2A, 2D, 2E) *H*

Avoids projecting one's own needs and limitations upon the other person. (2A, 2D, 2E) *H/P*

Displays an awareness of divergent cultural and ethnic traditions regarding suffering and death when interacting with the sick. (2A, 2B, 2D, 8H) *P*

Visits hospitals, nursing homes, prisons and homebound. (2A, 2B, 2D, 5F) *H/S*

Approaching Proficiency

Utilizes appropriate verbal and non-verbal communication in a clinical, hospice or home bound setting. (2A, 2D, 2E, 5F, 8H) *H*

Comforts others in need through presence, prayer and listening. (2A, 2B, 2C, 2D, 2E, 9A) *S/H*

Shows attention to the needs of individuals and families coping with tragic situations. (2A, 2B, 2D, 2E) *S/I/P*

Performance Area | Counsels Parishioners

Novice

Remains available and accessible for office appointments. (2B, 2C) H/P

Recognizes the human and spiritual needs of individuals and families. (2B, 2C, 2E, 3H) *S/I/P*

Integrates an awareness of family roles, customs and cultural dynamics relevant to those counseled in the guidance provided. (2B, 2C, 8H) *P/H/I*

Approaching Proficiency

Listens and provides feedback to help parishioners clarify issues and experiences through short term counseling. (2B) *I/P/H*

Avoids transference and upholds appropriate boundaries. (2B) *P/H*

Proficiency

Integrates the message of the Paschal mystery and witnesses to the hope of the Resurrection while attending to situations of suffering and death. (2A, 2D, 2E) *S/I*

Maintains a sense of belonging to the Christian community for parishioners in support groups or personal therapy. (2A, 2B, 2D) *P/I/S*

Above Proficiency

Provides continuing assistance for the marginalized and suffering. (2A, 2D) *P*

Inspires the parish community and others to respond to those in need. (2A, 2D, 3A, 3B, 4D, 7A) *P*

Proficiency

Identifies situations which call for referral to outside therapeutic or clinical services. (2B, 2D) *I*

Assists in discernment of the movement of grace in a person's life. (2B, 2C, 3G, 3H) *S/P*

Above Proficiency

Attains certification as a counselor. (2B, 8B) *I*

Provides Pastoral Care and Spiritual Guidance

Performance Area | **Offers Spiritual Direction and Retreats**

Novice	Approaching Proficiency
Gives spiritual talks and conferences. (2C, 3B, 3G) *I/S*	Introduces people to various models of spiritual growth and development. (2C, 3G) *I*
Provides clear explanation of spiritual direction. (2C, 3G) *I*	
Shares the Catholic spiritual tradition with the parish community. (2C, 3G, 3I) *I/P/S*	
Assists people through shared prayer in spiritual direction. (2C, 3H, 9A) *S/P*	

Performance Area | **Responds to Crisis Situations and Other Social Needs**

Novice	Approaching Proficiency
Empathizes with the plight and suffering of those in need. (2D, 2E, 2A) *H*	Sustains contact with those who are marginalized and suffering and helping them find the assistance that they need. (2D, 2E, 2A) *P*
Obtains the knowledge of parish, community resources, operational policies and contact people. (2D, 2E, 5A) *I*	Develops awareness of culturally specific social responses of people in need. (2D, 2E, 8H) *I/P*
Responds promptly and compassionately to those in need. (2D, 2E) *H/P*	

Performance Area | **Applies Canonical Procedures**

Novice	Approaching Proficiency
Works with canonical procedures and local diocesan policies. (2F, 4J) *P/I*	Identifies individuals in need of canonical assistance. (2F) *P/H*

Proficiency	Above Proficiency
Mentors people in their ongoing spiritual development. (2C, 2B, 3G, 3H) *S/I*	Gives retreats and parish missions. (2C, 3B, 3G, 3K) *S/H/I/P*
Gives days of recollection. (2C, 1H) *I/S/P*	Attains certification as a spiritual director. (2C, 8B) *S/H/I/P*

Proficiency	Above Proficiency
Organizes resources of the parish and local community/ government to respond to crisis situations. (2D, 4D, 5D, 7F) *P*	Develops new parish/ local community resources to respond to crisis situations as they occur. (2D, 2E, 7F) *P/I*
Provides language translators from needed professional services (e.g. legal counsel, immigration issues). (2D, 2E, 8H) *I/P*	Engages with a prophetic voice institutional and social structures that breed injustice and promotes more just structures. (2D, 2E, 7A) *P/I*
Makes referrals to social/community services. (2D, 2E) *P/H*	

Proficiency	Above Proficiency
Applies canonical requirements pastorally. (2F, 4J) *S/H/I/P*	Does further study in canon law. (2F, 8B) *I*
	Educates the community to the availability of canonical procedures (due process, annulment...) to assist them as needed. (2F, 3G) *P/I*

Teaches the Faith

Performance Area | **Evangelizes the Community and Culture**

Novice	Approaching Proficiency
Interprets the Catholic theological tradition accurately in a way accessible to contemporary culture. (3A, 3B, 8A, 8H) *I*	Evaluates culture in light of Catholic values (e.g. spiritual, sense of self-sacrifice, and awareness of community needs). (3A, 3B, 8H) *I/S/P*
	Exercises leadership role as evangelizer. (3A, 3B, 3I) *P/I*

Performance Area | **Models a Living Witness of the Gospel**

Novice	Approaching Proficiency
Maintains a standard of living appropriate to Gospel values. (3C, 9H) *S/H*	Works at personal ongoing conversion. (3C, 9A, 9B, 9C) *S/H*
Lives a chaste and celibate life and practices appropriate behavior in relationships. (3C, 9D) *S/H*	

Proficiency

Communicates the Catholic faith with sensitivity to the socio-economic, political, ethnic situations of the local community (culture). (3A, 3B, 8H) *I/H*

Such as:

> Trains lay people in techniques for sharing the Gospel in homes, workplaces, and neighborhood. (3B, 3G) *P/I*

> Dialogues with the doubters and unbelievers. (3B, 3H) *P*

> Promotes "Catholics Returning Home" programs by organizing effective outreach and developing programs. (3B, 4D) *P/S*

> Uses appropriate media to communicate the Catholic faith to a wider audience. (3A, 3B, 3I, 8H) *P/I*

Above Proficiency

Instills in the community a commitment to sharing the faith. (3A, 3B, 3G, 4D) *S/H/I/P*

Mediates the presence of Christ and the Church to the world by his personal presence, participation, interest, and encouragement. (3A, 3B, 3C, 5A, 5C, 5E) *S/H/I/P*

Proficiency

Inspires the practice of evangelical values by the community through personal example. (3C, 4D) *S/H*

Confronts social injustice through his actions that integrate Catholic values. (3C, 3B, 3I, 3J, 7A) *S/P*

Above Proficiency

Teaches the Faith

Performance Area | Implements RCIA Processes

Novice	**Approaching Proficiency**
Observes cues in people that indicate an interest in Catholicism and invites people to enter into the process of conversion. (3D) *S/I/H*	Ensures that the goals and values of RCIA are incorporated in the parish program. (3D, 4F) *I*
Ensures that qualified staff are in place who understand the RCIA process. (3D, 4F, 4G, 4I) *I*	Reviews, monitors the content and delivery of RCIA. (3D, 4F) *I*

Performance Area | Prepares People for Sacraments

Novice	**Approaching Proficiency**
Follows the guidelines in the National Directory of Catechesis (determines the readiness of the individual to receive the sacrament) for the preparation of sacraments. (3E, 3G) *I/P/S*	Instructs candidates and community in the fundamental historical and theological elements of the sacraments. (3E, 3G) *I/P*
Communicates the parish and diocesan guidelines (catechetical and canonical) for the preparation and reception of the sacraments. (3E, 3G) *P/I*	

Performance Area | Supervises Faith Formation Programs

Novice	**Approaching Proficiency**
Ensures the theological and pedagogical competency of the staff. (3F, 4F, 4I) *H/I*	Monitors and reviews programs. (3F, 4F, 4I) *I*
Prays and celebrates liturgy with faith formation staff. (3F, 9A) *S*	Supervises staff who share his responsibility for faith formation. (3F, 4F, 4I) *P*

Proficiency	**Above Proficiency**
Nurtures an environment of ongoing conversion (deepening of discipleship/spirituality/understanding of Catholic identity) within the parish community. (3D, 3A, 3B) *S/P/I*	Integrates a mystagogical dimension into the ongoing life of the parish. (3D) *S/H/I/P*
Draws the entire parish to RCIA at appropriate times in the liturgical year. (3D, 3A, 3B) *P/S*	Creates a family formation program. (3D) *S/H/I/P*

Proficiency	**Above Proficiency**
Adapts sacramental formation based on individual needs (age groups, cultural backgrounds, and SPRED groups). (3E, 8H) *P*	Offers presentations, courses and workshops on sacramental history and theology. (3E, 3G, 8A) *S/H/I/P*
Leads the parish community's ongoing sacramental formation. (3E, 3G) *P/I*	
Fosters the parish community's involvement in sacramental preparation. (3E, 3G) *P/I*	

Proficiency	**Above Proficiency**
Ensures that the full range of faith formation programs are in place and function effectively through regular dialogue among all those responsible for faith formation, opportunities for the ongoing formation (faith sharing) and development of staff. (3F, 4F, 4I) *I/P*	Establishes innovative, model programs for faith formation, and becomes a diocesan resource for faith formation programs. (3F) *S/H/I/P*
Provides ongoing guidance on theological and pastoral questions that emerge in faith formation programs. (3F, 3H, 4F, 4I) *I/P*	

Teaches the Faith

Performance Area | **Catechizes Adults, Youth, Children**

Novice	**Approaching Proficiency**
Able to identify the different learning needs and styles of various age levels. (3G) *I/H*	Utilizes opportunities to instruct various age groups. (3G) *I/H/P*

Performance Area | **Responds to Questions of Faith**

Novice	**Approaching Proficiency**
Makes himself approachable and welcomes questions of faith. (3H, 2C) *H/P*	Responds on matters of doctrine, tradition, and history with accuracy and understanding. (3H, 8A) *I/P*
Recognizes questioning as an opportunity for evangelization. (3H, 3B) *P*	Ascertains the level of background (age, degree of faith, level of understanding) of the questioner. (3H) *P/H*
Recommends appropriate resources (Catechism, Catholic Encyclopedia, Catholic online resources). (3H, 8A) *I*	

Performance Area | **Uses the Media to Communicate the Message of Faith**

Novice	**Approaching Proficiency**
Uses existing parish based media and other media sources for ongoing education on church practices and teaching. (3I, 3J) *P/I*	Explores the full range of media as new opportunities for communicating the faith. (3I, 3J) *H/P*

Proficiency	**Above Proficiency**
Provides for and uses age appropriate pedagogy in communicating the faith. (3G, 3I) *I/H*	Fulfills responsibility to be "the catechist of catechists" (role stated in National Directory for Catechesis). (3G) *P/I*

Proficiency	**Above Proficiency**
Allows questions from the faithful to guide his own personal reflection and pastoral application. (3H, 8E) *H/I/P* Provides insight into the practical and spiritual applications of doctrinal issues. (3H, 2C) *I/P/S*	Guides the questioner in further reflection and development of faith. (3H, 2C) *S/H/I/P* Provides opportunities for the community to probe questions of faith. (3H) *S/H/I/P*

Proficiency	**Above Proficiency**
Evaluates the full range of media for communicating the faith. (3I, 3J) *I/P* Incorporates appropriate media to communicate the faith. (3I, 3J, 8H) *I/P*	Develops new uses for media sources to communicate the faith. (3I, 3J, 8B) *I/P/S*

Leads Parish Administration

| Performance Area | Oversees Strategic Planning Grounded in Gospel Values and Diocesan Mission |

Novice	Approaching Proficiency
Drafts detailed strategic plans (goals, responsibilities, timelines). (4A, 4B) *I*	Participates in strategic planning at the parish level. (4A, 4B, 8G, 8H) *H/P/I*

| Performance Area | Leads Parish Pastoral and Finance Councils |

Novice	Approaching Proficiency
Enlists the expertise of consultative bodies within the parish. (4C, 4J, 4E, 4F, 8G) *I/H*	Chairs a project for one of the parish committees. (4C, 4J, 8G) *P/H*
Participates in various aspects of parish administrations (financial, personnel and physical plant management). (4C, 4J, 4E, 4G, 4H, 4I) *P/I*	Shares information regularly with committee chairs, council members and staff. (4C, 4J, 4F, 4I, 4K) *P/H*

| Performance Area | Oversees Parish Programs, Ministries and Apostolates |

Novice	Approaching Proficiency
Can identify the various programs, ministries and apostolates of the parish. (4F, 4D, 4J, 5A) *I/P*	Assesses the quality of existing parish programs, ministries and apostolates in light of local needs. (4F, 4J, 5A, 5D) *S/H/I/P*
Informs parish members of available ministries and apostolates. (4F, 4D, 4J, 5A) *P*	Promotes participation by calling parish members to share their time and talents. (4D) *P/S*
Keeps updated on diocesan policies and regulations. (4J) *I*	

Proficiency	Above Proficiency
Initiates a collaborative planning process using appropriate consultation, group dynamics, leadership styles and management techniques within an ecclesial framework. (4A, 4B, 4F, 4J, 7B, 8G, 8H) *I/P/S*	Serves as a consultant to other parishes for strategic planning. (4A, 4B, 6A, 8G, 8H) *S/H/I/P*
Oversees and monitors an evaluation process for the strategic plan. (4B, 4F) *I/P*	

Proficiency	Above Proficiency
Fulfills canonical and diocesan regulations for pastoral and financial councils. (4C, 4J) *S/H/I/P*	Inspires greater lay involvement in the councils and creativity with regard to stewardship in the parish. (4C, 4D) *S/H/I/P*
Sets goals in consultation with council members to guide their work in fulfilling the mission of the parish. (4C, 4F, 8G, 8H) *I/P*	Serves as a consultant on the diocesan level. (4J, 6A) *S/H/I/P*

Proficiency	Above Proficiency
Provides for the supervision and formation of parish staff, ministers and volunteers. (4D, 4J, 2C, 4I) *S/P/H*	Cultivates and nurtures a spirit of discipleship among parish ministers and staff. (4D, 4F, 2C, 4I) *S*
Organizes and promotes programs to carry out the mission of the Church. (4D, 4F, 7A) *P/S*	
Discerns the activity of God in the lives of people and calls them into various ministries and apostolates. (4D, 4F) *S/I/H*	
Coordinates (facilitates) communication among the various parish ministers, programs and apostolates. (4F, 5D, 8H) *P/H*	

Leads Parish Administration

Performance Area | **Oversees the Stewardship of Parish Finances**

Novice	Approaching Proficiency
Can identify and describe basic financial processes as they apply to the parish. (4E, 4J, 4C, 4I) *I*	Calls members of the parish to take responsibility for parish finances. (4E, 4J, 4C, 4D) *P/S*
Can read a financial statement and explain the parish budget. (4E, 4J, 4C, 4I) *I*	Utilizes the expertise of the parish financial council. (4E, 4J, 8G) *P*
Participates in workshops on diocesan financial policies and procedures. (4E, 4J, 4C, 4I, 8B) *I/P*	Aligns parish finances to meet all modifications/revisions in diocesan financial policies and procedures. (4E, 4J) *I/P*

Performance Area | **Employs and Manages Parish Staff**

Novice	Approaching Proficiency
Can describe basic diocesan personnel policies and procedures. (4G, 4I, 4J, 4H) *I*	Participates in the hiring process. (4G, 4J, 8G) *I/P*
Follows diocesan personnel policies and procedures. (4G, 4I, 4J, 4H) *I/P*	Writes job descriptions for parish staff openings. (4G, 4J) *I*
	Revises parish personnel policies and procedures in the light of changes in diocesan requirements. (4G, 4J) *I/P*

Proficiency	Above Proficiency
Prioritizes financial needs of the parish according to its mission. (4E, 4B, 4C, 8G) *P/S*	Creates endowment for parish operations and programs. (4E, 4J, 4D) *S/H/I/P*
Makes financial decisions following principles of good stewardship and gospel values. (4E, 4J, 4C, 4H, 8G) *P/S*	
Raises sufficient funds to carry out the mission of the parish. (4E, 4C, 4F, 4J) *I/P*	
Fulfills responsibilities of good stewardship according to diocesan policies. (4E, 4J) *S/H/I/P*	

Proficiency	Above Proficiency
Maintains a healthy work environment. (4I, 4J, 4F, 8G, 8H) *S/H*	Empowers staff to develop their full potential. (4I, 4J, 4D) *S/H/I/P*
Nurtures a spirit of discipleship among staff. (4I, 4J, 3C, 4F, 8G, 8H) *S*	
Makes personnel decisions following principles of good stewardship and gospel values. (4G, 4I, 4J, 3C, 8G, 8H) *P*	
Hires qualified individuals who support the needs/mission of the parish. (4G, 4J) *P*	
Reviews contracts and evaluates employees on a regular basis following diocesan policy (e.g. annually). (4I, 4J) *P*	
Mediates conflict among parish staff in keeping with diocesan policy, the parish mission and the good of the Church. (4I, 4J, 5G) *I/P/H*	
Provides for the supervision of staff. (4I, 4J, 8G) P/H/I	
Provides opportunities for continuing education of staff. (4I, 4J) *P/H/I*	

Leads Parish Administration

Performance Area | **Supervises the Maintenance of Physical Plant**

Novice	Approaching Proficiency
Can describe parish plant operations. (4H, 4J, 4I) *I*	Utilizes the expertise of the parish building and grounds committee. (4H, 4C, 8B) *P*
Develops working relationships with parish maintenance staff. (4H, 4J, 4I, 8H) *H/I*	Develops relationships with local businesses, unions and vendors. (4H) *H/I*
Participates in workshops on diocesan policies and canonical procedures regarding temporal goods. (4H, 4J, 4I, 8B) *I/P*	Appraises the effectiveness of physical plant operations. (4H) *I*

Performance Area | **Supervises Parish Communication**

Novice	Approaching Proficiency
Keeps updated on diocesan resources, memoranda and regulations. (4K, 4J) *I*	Develops a system for facilitating communication within the parish community. (4K, 4J, 5D, 8G) *I/H*
Assesses strengths and weaknesses of the various modes of communication available and in use in the parish (e.g. bulletin, web site, homily, mailings, announcements at Liturgy). (4K) *P/H*	

Proficiency	Above Proficiency
Exercises responsibility for physical facilities following principles of good stewardship and gospel values. (4H, 3C) *S/H/I/P*	Undertakes a building project. (4H, 4D) *S/H/I/P*
Sets goals in consultation with council members regarding the maintenance of physical facilities. (4H, 8G) *I/P*	Pursues efforts to upgrade plant with a sensitivity to protecting the environment. (4H, 4D) *S/H/I/P*
Creates plans to address emergency situations in consultation with appropriate staff. (4H, 8G) *I/P*	

Proficiency	Above Proficiency
Assures that parishioners are informed through various modes of communication (e.g. bulletin, web site, homily, mailings, announcements at Liturgy). (4K, 8H) *P/H*	Creates systems for communicating with larger publics. (4K, 4J, 3J, 7B) *H/I/P*
Maintains open communication both formally and informally (shares information with committee chairs, council members and staff, writes letters/emails/phone calls/meetings…) among various groups within the parish community. (4K, 4J, 5D, 8H) *P/H*	

Practices a Ministry of Presence with Parish Groups

Performance Area | **Participates with Individual Parish Groups**

Novice	Approaching Proficiency
Attends parish functions. (5A, 5C, 5E) *H/P*	Shows interest and concern for the work of the group and its members. (5A, 5C, 5E) *H/P*
Demonstrates appropriate etiquette, social graces/skills. (5A, 5C, 5E) *H*	Exhibits cultural sensitivities and authentic friendliness in interactions with families and groups. (5A, 5C, 5E, 5F, 8H) *H/I/P*

Performance Area | **Interacts with People in Informal Contexts**

Novice	Approaching Proficiency
Greets people before and after liturgy. (5B, 5F) *H*	Visits families' homes/dinners. (5F) *H/P*
Demonstrates appropriate etiquette, social graces/skills. (5B, 5F) *H*	Exhibits cultural sensitivities and authentic friendliness in interactions with families and groups. (5B, 5F, 8H) *H*

Performance Area | **Acts as Liaison Among Parish Groups**

Novice	Approaching Proficiency
Describes the purpose, mission and current activities of parish groups. (5D, 5A) *I/P*	Connects the purpose and mission of the individual groups to the parish and to each other. (5D, 5A) *H/P/I*

Proficiency	Above Proficiency
Listens and considers other perspectives. (5A, 5D, 5G) *H/I/P*	Mediates the presence of Christ and the Church to the world by his personal presence, participation, interest, and encouragement. (5A, 5C, 5D, 5E) *S/H/I/P*
Articulates his ideas and promotes effective cooperation in achieving the goals of the groups. (5A, 5D, 5E) *H/P*	
Communicates a sense of joy in being with parishioners. (5A, 5B, 5C, 5D, 5E) *H/P/S*	

Proficiency	Above Proficiency
Cultivates a personal presence of hospitality and warmth for all. (5B, 5F) *H/P*	Mediates the presence of Christ and the Church to the world by his personal presence, participation, interest, and encouragement. (5B, 5F) *S/H/I/P*
Seeks opportunities to establish and enhance a sense of community among parishioners. (5B, 5F) *P*	

Proficiency	Above Proficiency
Serves as an informed advisor on parish issues to parish groups and organizations in order to create unity. (5D, 5A) *I/P/S*	Mediates the presence of Christ and the Church to the world by his personal presence, participation, interest, and encouragement. (5D, 5A) *S/H/I/P*

Practices a Ministry of Presence with Parish Groups

Performance Area	Visits Schools/Religious Education (RE) Programs

Novice	Approaching Proficiency
Schedules time to spend with school and RE staff and students. (5E) *H*	Develops a relationship with the school and RE staff and students. (5E) *H/P*

Performance Area	Mediates Parish Conflicts

Novice	Approaching Proficiency
Identifies sources of conflict in individuals and groups. (5G, 2B, 2C, 2E, 4G, 5D, 7B, 7C) *I/P*	Listens and maintains open communication between all parish groups when disputes occur. (5G, 2B, 2C, 2E, 4G, 5D, 7B, 7C) *H/I/P*

Proficiency

Maintains a supportive relationship with the administration, teachers and staff of the school and/or religious educational program by fully participating in their efforts and events. (5E) *P/H*

Above Proficiency

Mediates the presence of Christ and the Church to the world by his personal presence, participation, interest, and encouragement. (5E) *S/H/I/P*

Proficiency

Applies appropriate strategies or processes to resolve conflicts. (5G, 2B, 2C, 2E, 4G, 5D, 7B, 7C) *H/I/P*

Initiates reconciliation between groups or individuals for successful resolution. (5G, 2B, 2C, 2E, 4G, 5D, 7B, 7C) *S/H/I/P*

Above Proficiency

Mediates the presence of Christ and the Church to the world by his personal presence, participation, interest, and encouragement. (5G, 2B, 2C, 2E, 4G, 5D, 7B, 7C) *S/H/I/P*

Participates in the Life of the Diocesan Church

Performance Area | Cooperates with Bishop

Novice	**Approaching Proficiency**
Respects the authority of the Bishop or his delegates in all matters of diocesan governance. (6A) *H/S/P*	Maintains a rapport with the Bishop through formal meetings and informal conversations (e.g. Presbyteral gatherings with priests, Confirmations). (6A, 6C, 6D, 6E) *H/S/P*
Employs a deep understanding of the nature and structure of the Church to establish relationships (with peers and superiors) and to guide actions. (6A, 4J, 6D, 6E, 6F) *I/P*	Implements diocesan policies and decisions. (e.g. Attends diocesan meetings, gives prompt attention to diocesan business.) (6A, 4J) *P/I*

Performance Area | Encourages Candidates for Church Ministries

Novice	**Approaching Proficiency**
Recognizes potential candidates for ministry by their personal gifts, evidence of spirituality and church involvement. (6B) *S/H*	Invites potential candidates to consider a call to ministry by naming the aspects of grace in their life. (6B) *S/H*
Offers information to those inquiring about discernment programs. (6B) *I/P*	

Proficiency

Incorporates a mindset of collaboration that presbyteral ministry is linked to the ministry of the Bishop (Reads, responds, implements diocesan memos; attends meetings with Bishop that relate to diocesan policies; attends workshops on liturgical procedures, responds to action statements that implement diocesan guidelines and policies). (6A, 6C, 6D, 6E) *H/S/P*

Initiates parish activities in conjunction with diocesan vision/ goals. (6A, 6F) *I/P*

Above Proficiency

Serves as a consultative resource for the Bishop. (6A) *S/H/I/P*

Leads projects in collaboration with the Bishop and all who minister in the local church. (6A, 6C) *S/H/I/P*

Proficiency

Supports candidates in their discernment by dialogue and by facilitating contact with vocation directors and diocesan personnel relating to ministry (Director of Diaconate Program, Lay Ecclesial Ministers Office). (6B) *H/S*

Above Proficiency

Maintains contact and support for candidates in formation programs. (6B) *S/H/I/P*

Participates in the Life of the Diocesan Church

Performance Area | **Collaborates with Presbyerate, Deacons, Religious and Lay Ecclesial Ministers**

Novice	Approaching Proficiency
Values the variety of church ministries and the process of collaboration. (6C, 6D, 6E) *H/I/P*	Demonstrates respect for the gifts and leadership of men and women engaged in various ministries. (6C, 6D, 6E, 8G) *H/P*

Performance Area | **Participates in Diocesan Administrative and Pastoral Structures**

Novice	Approaching Proficiency
Attends deanery/district meetings and appropriate presbyteral council events. (6D, 6E) *H/P*	Participates in the discussion and work of pastoral structures, demonstrating the skills of effective inquiry by asking questions, analyzing evidence, making informed judgments/decisions, and providing input on issues. (6D, 6E, 6F) *I/P*

Proficiency	**Above Proficiency**
Works harmoniously with all who minister in the local church in ways reflecting a proper theological and ecclesial understanding of their gifts and roles. (6C, 8G) *I*	Leads and mentors others in collaborative ministry. (6C, 8G) *S/H/I/P*

Proficiency	**Above Proficiency**
Takes responsibility for initiatives, policies and programs adopted by diocesan pastoral structures, communicating them to staff and parishioners. (6D, 6E, 6F) *P*	Exercises leadership at deanery and district levels by promoting such cooperation as is most beneficial for the diocesan Church. (6D, 6E, 6F) *S/H/I/P*

Engages With Diverse Publics

Performance Area | Promotes Community Outreach, Justice and Peace Programs

Novice

Provides referrals to the appropriate local community outreach program. (7A, 2D) *P*

Seeks information about the local community regarding justice and peace needs. (7A, 7D, 7F) *P*

Applies principles of Catholic social teaching to the pastoral context. (7A, 3J, 8A) *I/P*

Approaching Proficiency

Invites members of the parish community to engage in direct assistance to the community outreach programs and supplement them as needed. (7A, 3B, 4D) *P/H*

Dialogues with advocacy groups, such as fair housing alliance, etc. (7D, 7B, 3J) *P/H*

Performance Area | Builds Relationships with Diverse Cultural Groups

Novice

Seeks accurate information about the diverse cultural groups in the local and parish community. (7B) *I*

Develops multicultural sensitivity. (7B, 8I) *H/P*

Approaching Proficiency

Makes contact with the leaders of the various cultural communities. (7B, 7F, 8H) *P/H*

Creates an environment (liturgical, social, educational) that welcomes diverse groups. (7B, 8H) *P*

Proficiency

Preaches, teaches and models the principles of Catholic social teaching with passionate regard for those in need. (7A, 3A, 3B, 3C) *S/H/I/P*

Raises the consciousness of the parish community with regard to specific local, national and global issues of justice and peace. (7A, 3A, 3B, 3C, 4D) *S/H/I/P*

Recruits members of the parish community to engage in direct assistance to the community outreach programs and supplement them as needed. (7A, 3B, 3C, 4D) *P/H*

Above Proficiency

Leads advocacy groups (e.g. community employment, fair wages, fair housing, immigration) (7A, 3J, 7B, 7D) *S/H/I/P*

Serves on civic, religious and community boards. (7F) *S/H/I/P*

Proficiency

Incorporates examples from different cultural perspectives into preaching and teaching. (7B, 3A, 3B, 8H) *P*

Integrates the devotions and religious customs of the various cultural groups within the community into the life of the parish. (7B, 8H) *P*

Mediates tensions between different cultural groups. (7B, 5G, 8H) *P/I/H*

Above Proficiency

Creates strategies for intercultural dialogue and understanding. (7B, 8H) *P/H*

Speaks the language(s) of the parish community. (7B, 8H) *I*

Engages With Diverse Publics

Performance Area	Mediates Theologically Diverse Intra-ecclesial Perspectives

Novice	Approaching Proficiency
Engages in critical self-reflection to detect and avoid ideological bias. (7C, 8A, 8E) *S/I*	Uses resources and personnel to introduce the parish community to a range of authentic theological perspectives. (7C, 8A) *I/P*

Performance Area	Engages in Ecumenical and Interfaith Dialogue and Activity

Novice	Approaching Proficiency
Cultivates respect for other religious traditions in preaching, teaching. (7E, 3A, 8H) *S/H/I/P* Uses various resources to inform the parish community about the principles of ecumenical and interfaith dialogue, (e.g. library and magazine rack). (7E) *P/I*	Promotes the Week of Prayer for Christian Unity in the parish. (7E) *P*

Proficiency	Above Proficiency
Uses mediation skills and practices to achieve reconciliation among groups in conflict. (7C, 5G) *S/H/I/P*	
Integrates a range of Catholic theological perspectives in teaching and preaching. (7C, 5G, 8A) *S/H/I/P*	

Proficiency	Above Proficiency
Sponsors ecumenical and interfaith services and projects. (7E) *I/P/S*	Participates in diocesan ecumenical/ interfaith commission. (7E, 6C, 6D, 6E) *S/H/I/P*
Provides educational opportunities for the parish to learn about other faith traditions. (7E) *P/I*	
Participates in local ecumenical and interfaith groups. (7E) *P/H*	

Engages in Professional Development

Performance Area | Maintains a Habit of Theological Reading and Reflection

Novice	Approaching Proficiency
Subscribes to various theological journals and homiletic resources (e.g. liturgical, pastoral, ministerial, scriptural). (8A) *I*	Maintains a personal library of current theological reading materials that will promote professional advancement. (8A) *I*
Attends classes/ seminars. (8A, 8B) *I*	Develops a system for recording theological ideas for subsequent use. (8A) *I*
Schedules time for reading and reflection. (8A) *I*	

Performance Area | Acquires New Skills for Ministry

Novice	Approaching Proficiency
Assesses personal gifts and needed skills for ministry. (8B, 8D, 8E) *H/I/P*	Acquires administrative skills in parish leadership. (8B, 8D) *P/H*
Participates in workshops/seminars as a part of continuing education. (8B) *I*	Consults with peers and experts to hone ministerial skills. (8B, 8D) *I*

Performance Area | Engages in Ministerial Self-evaluation on a Regular Basis

Novice	Approaching Proficiency
Welcomes feedback from parishioners, peers, neutral parties. (8E, 8D) *H*	Monitors growth in relation to all four pillars of priestly formation (Human, Spiritual, Intellectual, Pastoral). (8E, 9B) *H*
Identifies personal stressors, conflicts, compulsions (compulsive behaviors) and acts to address them. (8E) *H*	Seeks and uses constructive criticism from parishioners for growth in pastoral skills (homilies, liturgical style, leadership skills). (8D, 8E, 4C) *H/S*
Consults with mentors, peers and experts regarding pastoral practices. (8D, 8E) *P*	
Utilizes self-help materials/ action steps to regulate personal growth and progress. (8D, 8E) *H/S*	

Proficiency	**Above Proficiency**
Discusses salient ideas and views with colleagues. (8A, 8D) *I*	Publishes or presents the fruits of theological reflection at a local or national level. (8A, 8F) *S/H/I/P*
Applies theological ideas to pastoral, social and cultural situations. (8A, 2B, 3B, 7A) *I/P/H*	Researches and identifies best pastoral practices and strategies. (8A, 8B) *I*

Proficiency	**Above Proficiency**
Obtains proper credentials to work in specialized ministries (8B) *I*	Mentors/teaches others. (8B, 8F) *S/H/I/P*
Develops advanced language skills for ministerial outreach to ethnic communities. (8B, 8H) *I*	
Utilizes newly acquired skills. (8B) *S/H/I/P*	

Proficiency	**Above Proficiency**
Initiates periodic formal reviews to evaluate ministerial abilities and gifts (e.g. peers, parishioners). (8D, 8E, 4C) *H*	Takes advantage of opportunities for advanced training to improve ministerial skills as a result of self-evaluation and feedback. (8E, 8B) *S/H/I/P*
Maintains a commitment to participate regularly in a priest support group. (8D, 8E) *H/S*	

Engages in Professional Development

Performance Area	Contributes to Development of the Profession

Novice	Approaching Proficiency
	Serves on diocesan councils and/or committees. (8F) *I/P*
	Forms a priest support group. (8F, 8C) *H/P/S*

Performance Area	Develops a Collaborative Leadership Style

Novice	Approaching Proficiency
Can identify traits, strengths and weaknesses of personal leadership style. (8G, 8E) *H/P/I*	Works to eliminate personal behaviors detrimental to collaboration. (8G, 8E, 9B) *H/P/I*
Recognizes the gifts and talents of others in ministry. (8G) *I/P*	
Consults others. (8G, 8D) *P/H*	
Shares leadership by delegating responsibility. (8G) *P*	

Proficiency

Shares skills from advanced degrees, or previous profession, with the wider diocesan community. (8F) *I/P*

Provides assistance to the presbyterate from an area of expertise. (8F) *I/P*

Serves as mentor to newly ordained, seminary field education supervisor or adjunct faculty. (8F) *I/P*

Above Proficiency

Makes self available to mentor other clergy, parishes. (8F) *I/P*

Shares expertise through a variety of media to larger audiences. (8F, 3I) *I/P/S/H*

Serves as a spiritual director to priests. (8F) *S*

Proficiency

Works with others showing respect for diverse ministries and professional skills of others. (8G) *H/P*

Above Proficiency

Teaches and mentors others to develop a more collaborative style of leadership. (8G, 8F) *I/P*

Engages in Personal Development

Performance Area | **Deepens Spiritual Life**

Novice

Prays daily the Liturgy of the Hours, privately or in common. (9A) *S*

Schedules quiet time for self-reflection and engages in private meditation on a daily basis. (9A, 8E) *S*

Does spiritual reading. (9A) *S*

Receives the Sacrament of Reconciliation on a regular basis. (9A) *S*

Receives spiritual direction on a regular basis. (9B) *S*

Participates in yearly retreat. (9C) *S*

Engages in devotional prayer (e.g. prays rosary, Stations of the Cross, Novenas). (9A) *S*

Approaching Proficiency

Prays with others. (9A) *S*

Performs ministerial activities informed by a spirit of prayer. (9A) *S/P*

Uses self-critical skills to address obstacles in prayer with spiritual director. (9B, 8E) *S/H*

Resolves and reconciles anxieties, fears and failures through disclosure with a mentor, or through self-examination and the sacrament of reconciliation. (9B, 8E) *S/H*

Engages in introspection regarding one's life in ministry. (9B, 8E) *S/H/P*

Performance Area | **Maintains Physical and Mental Health**

This performance area does not warrant a division into levels of mastery. This does not diminish its importance. Below is a sample checklist of performance statements that demonstrate success in the performance area:

[ ]   Exercises on weekly basis (e.g. goes to gym, bikes, jogs). (9E) *H*

[ ]   Engages in recreational, cultural and social activities. (9E, 9F, 9G) *H*

[ ]   Gets a yearly physical. (9E) *H*

[ ]   Follows a healthy diet, maintains appropriate weight. (9E) *H*

[ ]   Avoids compulsive behaviors. (9E) *H*

[ ]   Recognizes and acts on warning signs of depression. (9E) *H*

[ ]   Seeks professional help when needed. (9E) *H*

[ ]   Gets an adequate amount of sleep. (9E) *H*

Proficiency	Above Proficiency
Remains faithful to spiritual practices as a priority. (9A, 9B, 9C, 8E) *S/H*	Serves as a spiritual director. (9A, 8F) *S/H*
Integrates insights from spiritual direction into preaching and pastoral care. (9B, 2B, 3A) *S/P*	
Utilizes insights from spiritual direction to discern direction in ministry. (9B, 8E) *S/P*	
Uses prayer to guide goals, desires and personal needs as a minister. (9A, 8E) *S/P*	

Engages in Personal Development

| Performance Area | **Maintains Balance in Life and Ministry** |

This performance area does not warrant a division into levels of mastery. This does not diminish its importance. Below is a sample checklist of performance statements that demonstrate success in the performance area:

[   ]   Visits or calls family (parents) on a regular basis. (9D) *H*

[   ]   Nurtures healthy friendships (family/ friends). (9D) *H*

[   ]   Socializes with priests and friends through dinners, vacations, days off to allow for the development of friendships. (9D) *H*

[   ]   Participates in a priest support group. (9D, 8C) *H/S*

[   ]   Develops effective systems of personal organization and time management. (9F) *S/H*

[   ]   Manages personal and work schedules and commitments to meet ministerial obligations and maintain a healthy life style. (9F, 9G) *H*

[   ]   Takes days off and yearly vacations. (9G) *H*

[   ]   Manages personal finances. (9H) *H/I*

[   ]   Lives within the limits of the presbyteral salary structure. (9H) *H*

[   ]   Invests money for retirement. (9H) *H/I/P*

[   ]   Contributes to charities. (9H) *H/P*

[   ]   Makes a commitment to stewardship. (9H) *H/P*

The Use of an Assessment Portfolio in Seminary Formation

In this new era of performance assessment related to the monitoring of students' mastery of a core curriculum, faculty are turning to the use of portfolios as a means of revealing the full range of student skills and understanding.

A portfolio is a purposeful collection of student work that exhibits student efforts, progress, and achievements in one or more areas of a curriculum. The collection typically includes student participation in selecting assignments that reflect the breadth and depth of the degree program and guidelines to aid students in selecting their best work. Faculty use objective criteria to evaluate student performance as evidenced by the assignments and take into account student self-reflection.[1]

The MATS panel involved in the creation of *In Fulfillment of Their Mission* and its scoring rubrics have considered the advantages of adopting portfolios as an assessment tool at their institutions. They note that both seminarians and faculty stand to benefit from adoption of portfolio assessment. In the view of the panel:

For Seminarians—Portfolios can enlarge the educational experience of students because they place greater responsibility upon learners to determine how best to demonstrate their learning. Portfolios encourage seminarians to engage in self reflection and to take full ownership of their education and formation.

Seminarians are accountable for all aspects of priestly formation within the parameters of the external forum. This includes participation in spiritual exercises, the spiritual direction program, liturgical exercises, and community life as well as the academic and pastoral dimensions of priestly formation. This approach is taken because all the aspects of priestly formation are "intimately interwoven and should not be separated from one another."[2]

Portfolios offer students a means by which they can document and track their progress toward clearly identified outcomes. The examples of evidence collected for inclusion in a portfolio provide indications of pastoral viability, personal and spiritual integration that are not solely visible by academic skills alone. At the same time, the flexibility inherent in the portfolio approach allows it to be adapted to meet specific performance skill sets within the curriculum (e.g. liturgical practica, and homiletics). In addition, writing samples of academic work in scripture, dogmatic theology, church history and sacramental theology allow students to articulate doctrinal formulations while recognizing contemporary modes of theological expression and explanation through specific venues that require synthesis, analysis and pastoral application.[3] For seminarians whose first language is not English, portfolios can establish an even playing field with other students.

---

[1] Paulson, F.L. Paulson, P.R. and Meyer, C.A. (1991, February). "What Makes a Portfolio a Portfolio?" *Educational Leadership*, pp. 60-63.

[2] Program of Priestly Formation (2006, Fifth Edition) United States Conference of Catholic Bishops Paragraph 275, p.90

[3] Ibid. paragraph 225, p.75.

For Seminary Faculty—Portfolios can also enlarge the perspective of faculty members. Seminarian portfolios provide faculty a more robust means of assessing their students, and can stimulate a shift in seminary culture. They prompt instructors to move away from an emphasis on grades and individual courses to a stronger regard for an overall composite of student learning. This is because portfolios naturally encourage the integration of skills and knowledge across subject areas. As a result, instructors are inclined to move beyond an isolated, departmental perspective towards a deeper awareness of the whole program of formation. At the same time, portfolios offer evidence to accrediting institutions that seminaries are doing what they claim to be doing.

The use of *In Fulfillment of Their Mission* as a portfolio model

Portfolios can easily be used for outcomes assessment of individual students as well as summative assessment of the group of graduates in a particular year. Outcomes assessment is summative assessment which occurs at the end of the learning process. It assesses components within a degree to which students have achieved the stated learning goals (or outcomes). This type of assessment is cohort driven because it examines the learning artifacts of a specific group of students in order to understand the degree to which that group has achieved the mastery of skills, objectives and goals within a particular program. The Master of Divinity degree "takes into account knowledge of religious heritage; understanding of the cultural context; growth in spiritual depth and moral integrity; and the capacity for ministerial and public leadership."[4] These multi-layered qualities, goals, traits and skills become the criteria for students and faculty to use as specific benchmarks.

The sample elements based on *In Fulfillment of their Mission* provide a good example of how portfolio assessment can guide seminaries to collect examples of evidence from students. Using specific performance areas related to specific duties, examples are provided using various assessment models and methods to retrieve learning artifacts from students. This is done by using specific courses within a given year of formation and the many reviewers associated with a seminary community that may be able to provide concrete feedback. At times, examples of specific projects that illustrate best practices have been included.

---

[4] The Association of Theological Schools Bulletin 47 (2006): A.2 Primary Goals of the Program, p.191

SAMPLE ELEMENTS OF A SEMINARIAN PORTFOLIO

DUTY ONE

Celebrates Liturgy and Sacraments

Performance Areas Related to Duty	Examples of Evidence to be Reviewed
– Celebrates the Eucharist	– Video tape celebrating the rite
– Preaches liturgical homilies	– Sample of written homily
– Initiates children and adults	– Feedback from mentor/congregation (e.g. surveys, Likert scales, focus group)
– Celebrates sacraments of healing	– Preparation journals that incorporate goals for preaching and feedback (e.g. social analysis, exegesis, pastoral application)
– Officiates at weddings	
– Celebrates funerals	– Written feedback on role play for practica (e.g. reconciliation, weddings)
– Leads devotional practices	– Self-reflection papers
– Coordinates liturgical events and training	– Written and/or oral feedback from pastoral supervisors and lay boards
	– Observation checklists completed by faculty
	– Listing in seminary catalog/bulletin of homiletic study group organized by students
	– Schedule, topics and participant lists of student-created support groups
	– Web blog of stories and anecdotes to be developed into homilies

Courses and Other Learning Experiences	Reviewers of Evidence

Courses

– Sacramental Theology with Practica

– Liturgical Leadership

– Homiletics

– Liturgical Planning

Other learning experiences

– Internships

– Theological Field Education

– Exercise of Diaconal Ministry

– Formation Conferences

– Faculty

– Formators

– Pastoral supervisors

– Lay boards

– Lay people

– Peers

DUTY TWO

Provides Pastoral Care and Spiritual Guidance

Performance Areas Related to Duty	Examples of Evidence to be Reviewed
– Visits the sick and others in need	– Feedback from supervisor's reports
– Counsels parishioners	– Video and audio tapes of counseling practica
– Offers spiritual direction and retreats	– Theological reflection reports, verbatims, case studies…
– Responds to crisis situations and other social needs	– Written testimonials
– Applies canonical procedures	– Commendations
	– Self-reflection journals
	– Personality inventory
	– Record of completion of Virtus training
	– Observation checklists
	– Formation reports
	– Copy of learning contract/agreement on pastoral activities
	– Case reports of canonical procedures
	– Agendas/reports/brochures/posters of pastoral events/activities organized/conducted by students
	– Certificate of completion of online course(s)

Courses and Other Learning Experiences

Courses

- Pastoral Theology

- Pastoral Counseling

- Canon Law

- Sacramental Theology

- Marriage

- Moral Theology

- Philosophy

- Spirituality

Other learning experiences

- Clinical Pastoral Education Placement

- Field Education

- Virtus workshops

- Spiritual Direction

- Internships

- Tribunal Internship

Reviewers of Evidence

- Faculty

- Formators

- Pastoral supervisors

- Lay boards

- Lay people

- Peers

- Diocesan personnel

DUTY THREE

Teaches the Faith

Performance Areas Related to Duty

- Evangelizes the community and culture

- Models a living witness of the Gospel

- Implements RCIA processes

- Prepares people for sacraments

- Supervises faith formation programs

- Catechizes adults, youth, children

- Responds to questions of faith

- Uses the media to communicate the message of faith

Examples of Evidence to be Reviewed

- Field education supervisor report

- Lesson plans for RCIA, bible studies, sacramental preparation

- Selected academic papers

- Debrief notes/report from teaching mentor

- Capstone project

- Designed catechetical web page and/or blogs

- Written feedback from RCIA team and participants

- Report on leadership activities during summer bible camp

- Articles written for parish and/or diocesan bulletins

- Electronic presentations of talks given (e.g. Theology on Tap, mission experiences)

- Reports on activities organized to raise funds for social justice work

- Agendas/bulletins of events/conferences organized for peers at other seminaries

- Reports from formators

- Peer reviews

- Photographs of participation in social justice activities

- Evaluation forms completed by students in catechetical classes

Courses and Other Learning Experiences

Courses

- Pastoral Theology

- Sacramental Theology

- Moral Theology

- Philosophy

- Electronic (Media) Communication

- Spirituality

- Ecclesiology

- Missiology

- Christology

- Catechetics

    Fundamental Theology

- Trinitarian Theology

- Theological Anthropology

- Sacred Scripture

Other learning experiences

- Field Education

- Teaching Practicum

- Mission experiences

- Summer bible camp

- Internships

- Theological Reflection

Reviewers of Evidence

- Faculty

- Formators

- Pastoral supervisors

- Lay boards

- Lay people

- Peers

- Mission personnel

- Teachers in schools and/or RE programs who serve as mentors

- IT director/instructors

- Students in catechetical classes

Examples of Projects

- Designs/develops/produces products to support the parish strategic communication plan.

- Reviews and offers revisions of parish RCIA program.

- Designs and facilitates an adult faith formation series.

DUTY FOUR

Leads Parish Administration

Performance Areas Related to Duty	Examples of Evidence to be Reviewed
– Oversees strategic planning grounded in Gospel values and diocesan mission	– Field education supervisor report
– Leads parish pastoral and finance councils	– Evaluation of Leadership in Administration course (e.g. strategic planning, budget)
– Oversees parish programs, ministries and apostolates	– Leadership skills self-report
– Overseas the stewardship of parish finances	– Case studies solving pastoral issues/problems
– Employs and manages parish staff	– Work history evidence of administrative and management experience (former employers)
– Supervises maintenance of physical plant	
– Supervises parish communication	

Courses and Other Learning Experiences	Reviewers of Evidence

Courses

- Canon Law course on temporal goods

- Leadership

- Pastoral Skills

- Parish Administration

- Workshops on stewardship

Other learning experiences

- Pastoral Internship

- Formation sessions

- Presentations by diocesan personnel

- Visits to diocesan offices

- Workshops on stewardship

- Ecclesiology of local church and parish

- Integrating Seminar

- Capstone project

Reviewers of Evidence

- Internship supervisor

- Faculty

- Formators

- Pastoral supervisors

- Lay boards

- Lay people

- Peers

- Diocesan personnel

- Pastors

- Consultants/specialists

Practices a Ministry of Presence with Parish Groups

Performance Areas Related to Duty	Examples of Evidence to be Reviewed
– Participates with individual parish groups	– Roster/attendance logs of participation in multi-cultural committee(s)
– Interacts with people in informal contexts	– Verbatim of participation in popular religious devotions
– Acts as liaison among parish groups	– Field education supervisor report
– Visits schools/religious education (RE) programs	– Internship report
– Mediates parish conflicts	– Report from school principal
	– Video tape of role play of resolving conflicts in parish skills course
	– Parishioner surveys
	– Photographs of interactions in informal gatherings
	– Newspaper articles/photos of events
	– Written theological reflection (e.g. on importance of silence/listening)
	– CPE reports/verbatims
	– Formation reports on student involvement in community life
	– Internship contract

Courses and Other Learning Experiences

Courses

– Parish Skills

– Pastoral Counseling

– Pastoral Leadership

– Theological Reflection

Other learning experiences

– Field Practica (e.g. CPE, Internships)

– Formation sessions

– Seminars on conflict resolution/mediation

– Experiences of providing hospitality in the seminary (e.g. tours of seminary, holiday parties)

Reviewers of Evidence

– Internship supervisor

– Faculty

– Formators

– Pastoral supervisors

– Lay boards

– Lay people

– Peers

– Pastors

– Ministry readiness (or other designated) committee

– Vocation directors

– Bishop

Examples of Projects

– Starts a social club in a parish

– Researches project on seating patterns in church (sociogram).

Participates in the Life of the Diocesan Church

Performance Areas Related to Duty	Examples of Evidence to be Reviewed
– Cooperates with Bishop	– Serves as MC for Bishop
– Encourages candidates for church ministries	– Notes from vocation director on vocation talks
– Collaborates with presbyterate, deacons, religious and lay ecclesial ministers	– Minutes/notes indicating attendance as liaison of seminary to Presbyteral Council
– Participates in Diocesan Administrative and Pastoral Structures	– Photographs from diocesan newspapers
	– Attendance lists from diocesan convocations and Presbyteral days
	– Internship reports indicating participation in activities of the diocese
	– Reports from vocation director indicating participation in diocesan life

Courses and Other Learning Experiences

Courses

– Diocesan Church History

– Ecclesiology

– Canon Law

– Leadership in Administration

Other learning experiences

– Field trips/visits to parishes and other churches

– Interviews with diocesan clergy

– Bishop/student meetings/dialogs

– Formation sessions

– Personnel board meetings/conversations

– Meetings with Vicar of Clergy

Reviewers of Evidence

– Internship supervisor

– Faculty

– Formators

– Pastoral supervisors

– Lay boards

– Lay people

– Peers

– Pastors

– Ministry readiness (or other designated) committee

– Vocation directors

– Bishop

– Chancery officials

Examples of Projects

– Hosts a social gathering for Presbyterate and seminarians (e.g. social event honoring retired priest).

– Organizes high school vocational discernment weekend retreat.

DUTY SEVEN

Engages with Diverse Publics

Performance Areas Related to Duty	Examples of Evidence to be Reviewed
– Promotes community outreach, justice and peace programs	– Project report on various service agencies and referral processes
– Builds relationships with diverse cultural groups	– Brochure of activities for Week of Prayer for Christian Unity
– Mediates theologically diverse intra-ecclesial perspectives	– Reports on cultural immersion experiences
– Engages in ecumenical and interfaith dialogue and activity	– Field education reports from social justice placements (e.g. visits to sick, volunteer work in soup kitchen)
	– Photographs/attendance records of participation in social justice marches/activities (e.g. Pro-Life, immigration reform)
	– Transcript of interviews with ministers and religious leaders from other bodies of faith
	– Reports/reflections on visits to services of other denominations/religions
	– Reports/reflections on participation in multi-cultural events
	– Supervisor report on work with Diocesan Ecumenical and Interfaith office, Offices for Women's Concerns, African- Asian-Hispanic Ministries

Courses and Other Learning Experiences

Courses

- Church History

- Catholic Social Teaching

- Culture and Religion

- Immersion courses in language and culture

- Catholic Identity Studies

- Popular Religiosity

- African-Asian-Hispanic American Studies

Other learning experiences

   Ecumenism and Interfaith Dialogue

- Internship

- Diocesan Ecumenical and Interfaith office

- Catholic Charities

- Social Justice

- Pilgrimage experience(s)

- Exchange programs

- Cross registration with other seminaries

Reviewers of Evidence

- Internship supervisor

- Faculty

- Formators

- Pastoral supervisors (director social service agency)

- Lay boards

- Lay people

- Peers

- Pastors

- Vocation directors

- Chancery officials

Examples of Projects

- Translates parish documents into bilingual formats that are culturally inviting to parishioners.

- Establishes parish committees to respond to diverse culture/language issues facing the parish.

- Sponsors liturgies for special populations, (e.g. hearing impaired, African-American, Hispanic).

- Develops a class for the seminary community in specific languages for liturgical celebrations.

- Participates in and reports back to seminary on relevant conferences/ workshops from the National Pastoral Life Center and/or others such as the Common Ground Initiative.

- Organizes campaign on campus to sensitize seminary to women's issues.

Engages in Professional Development

Performance Areas Related to Duty	Examples of Evidence to be Reviewed
– Maintains a habit of theological reading and reflection	– Self assessment identifying skill needs
– Acquires new skills for ministry	– Written seminary and ongoing formation plans
– Engages in ministerial self-evaluation on a regular basis	– Written connections between professional development needs to the profile *In Fulfillment of Their Mission*
– Contributes to development of the profession	– Certifications of new languages learned for ministry
– Develops a collaborative leadership style	– Certifications of new skill sets (e.g. technology)
	– Memberships in professional organizations
	– Annual self evaluations
	– Attendance records of seminary sponsored support/ development programs (e.g. newly ordained priest, new pastors, sabbatical programs)
	– Papers submitted for publication in theological journals
	– Subscriptions to journals and homiletic resources
	– Written reflections on case studies for collaboration
	– Field education reports on collaborative leadership style
	– Completed evaluation/tools on leadership style Courses

Courses and Other Learning Experiences

Courses

– Pastoral Skills

– Administrative Leadership

– Theology of Priesthood

– Spanish, Hmong, Vietnamese, Tagalog....

– Seminars

– Workshops

– Online courses

Other learning experiences

– Internship

– Formation sessions

Reviewers of Evidence

– Internship supervisor

– Faculty

– Formators

– Pastoral supervisors

– Lay boards

– Lay people

– Peers

– Pastors

– Vocation directors

– Bishop

– Editorial boards

Examples of Projects

– Creates website, webcasts/podcasts on topics of interest to share with peers.

– Leads Online dialogs/blogs on collaborative leadership styles and issues in the church.

– Assists Diocesan Office of Professional Evaluation.

– Organizes reading and discussion groups on theological topics, language conversation groups.

Engages in Personal Development

Performance Areas Related to Duty	Examples of Evidence to be Reviewed
— Deepens spiritual life	— Written attendance report from spiritual director
— Maintains physical and mental health	— Attendance in spiritual formation sessions, annual retreats, Health and Wellness Committees
— Maintains balance in life and ministry	— Human formation reports
	— Completed health and wellness assessments/tools
	— Itinerary of vacations and leisure time activities
	— Calendar book that includes time for relaxation, exercise, wellness activities, support groups and work
	— Written personal financial plan
	— Copies of sign/out book that indicates time spent with family
	— Fitness progress charts/exercise logs
	— Completed rubric checklist based on Duty 9 of the priest profile.

Courses and Other Learning Experiences

Courses

- Parish skills

- Seminars

Other learning experiences

- Formation sessions (intellectual, human, spiritual, pastoral)

Reviewers of Evidence

- Faculty

- Formators

- Pastoral supervisors

- Pastors

- Vocation directors

- Bishop

Examples of Projects

- Organizes a health and wellness committee on campus.

- Raises funds and secures equipment to maintain gym facility on campus.

- Starts spiritual fraternity group.

- Organizes sport teams/activities.

- Participates in leagues, sports activities in neighboring colleges.

- Organizes marathons with area colleges.

- Creates an individual development plan based on the priest profile/rubrics.

APPENDIX A
The Successful Priest – Skills and Knowledge

SKILLS IN:

Communication
    Public speaking
    Writing
    Listening
    Cross cultural relations

Computer use

Homiletics

Interpersonal relations
    Collaboration

Leadership
    Presiding
    Decision-making
    Governance
    Budgetary oversight

Organization
    Human resources
    Time management

Pastoral Care
    Counseling

Practices
    Conflict mediation

Pedagogy
    moral

Problem Solving

Theological reflection
    Research

KNOWLEDGE OF:

Adult learning theory

Canon law

Catechetics

Church history

Comparative religion

Contemporary culture

Diocesan structures

Family dynamics

Group dynamics

Legal knowledge

Multicultural Church

Politics

Professional ethics

Scripture

Second languages

Self reflection practices

Social justice issues

Social service resources

Spiritual direction

Theology
    (systematic, spiritual, liturgical,
    sacramental, pastoral)

Western philosophy

Appendix B
The Successful Priest – Behaviors and Attributes
The Successful Priest is . . .

A critical thinker

Able to accept criticism

Able to compromise

Able to delegate

Able to laugh

Able to make unpopular decisions

Able to weigh alternatives

Balanced

Collaborative

Committed to service

Compassionate

Creative

Disciplined in study habits

Empathetic

Enthusiastic

Flexible

Generous

Globally conscious

Gracious

Grateful

Hard working

Honest

Hospitable

Humble

Intellectually curious

Joyful

Judicious

Logical

Morally upright

Multi-task oriented

Non-judgmental

Observant of professional boundaries

Optimistic

Passionate

Prayerful

Punctual

Reflective

Respectful

Respectful of the institutional Church

Responsible

Self-confident

Self-critical

Sensible

Warm

Appendix C
Resources for Priests

– A good professional library (subscriptions to relevant journals, homily resources, reference materials, liturgical books, canon law)

– Clerical attire

– Office equipment/supplies including phone, cell phone, computer (networked), copy machine, fax machine.

– Office space

– Office space for confidential conversations

– Car

– Appointment book/pda

– Liturgical resources

– Instructional resources (e.g. videos)

– Specialized phone lists (e.g. social services…)

– Street maps/navigation equipment/supplies

– Appropriate software (compatible with diocese)

– Diocesan procedural manuals

– Access to exercise equipment

Appendix D
Defining the Current Context of the Ministry

– Decreasing number of clergy

– Recruitment issues regarding the profession

– Declining financial resources

– Declining participation in the Church

– Growing the membership of the parish

– Ministering to changing family dynamics

– Changing demographics of U.S. Catholic Church population (e.g. Hispanic/African/Asian)

– Youth's increased interest in the Church

– Consolidated parishes

– Multiple parish responsibilities

– Growing number of lay ministers

– Increasing number of permanent deacons

– Co-responsibility with lay leadership

– Changed relationship with the ordinary (Bishop)

– Intergenerational conflicts in presbyterates

– Diminished professional image of the priesthood

– Impact of sexual abuse scandal on future Church ministry

– Increasing number of international clergy

– Shift away from a Eurocentric view of the Church

– Justice issues in Church employment (salary, health benefits, retirement)

– Continuing gulf between reality and potentiality of women's place in the Church

– New religious movements

DUTIES	TASKS				
1 Celebrates Liturgy and Sacraments	1A Celebrates Eucharist	1B Preaches liturgical homilies	1C Initiates children and adults (Baptism, Confirmation, Eucharist)	1D Celebrates Reconciliation	1E Officiates at weddings
2 Provides Pastoral Care and Spiritual Guidance	2A Visits the sick and others in need	2B Counsels parishioners	2C Offers spiritual direction	2D Provides assistance or referrals to social/ community services	2E Responds to crisis situations
3 Teaches the Faith	3A Preaches the Gospel	3B Evangelizes the community and culture	3C Models a living witness of the Gospel	3D Implements RCIA processes	3E Prepares people for sacraments
4 Leads Parish Administration	4A Initiates strategic planning (vision/ goals/programs)	4B Oversees implementation of strategic plan	4C Participates in parish, pastoral and finance councils	4D Animates parish ministries, apostolates and volunteers	4E Oversees parish finance (e.g. budget, fundraising diocesan assessment. . .)
5 Practices a Ministry of Presence with Parish Groups	5A Participates in parish groups (e.g. youth, older adults, divorced, bereaved . . .)	5B Greets people before and after liturgy	5C Attends parish functions	5D Acts as liaison among parish groups	5E Visits schools/religious education (RE) programs
6 Participates in the Life of the Diocesan Church	6A Cooperates with Bishop	6B Encourages priestly/ religious vocations and lay ministry	6C Collaborates with presbyterate, deacons, religious and lay ecclesial ministers	6D Interacts with Presbyteral Council	6E Attends deanery/district meetings
7 Engages with Diverse Publics	7A Promotes community outreach, justice and peace programs (e.g. shelters/food pantries)	7B Builds relationships with diverse cultural groups	7C Mediates theologically diverse intra-ecclesial perspectives	7D Participates in advocacy groups (e.g. Pax Christi, pro-life, death penalty, save the children, immigration reform. . .)	7E Engages in ecumenical and interfaith dialogue and activity
8 Engages in Professional Development	8A Maintains a habit of theological reading and reflection	8B Acquires new skills for ministry	8C Participates in a priest support group	8D Consults with mentor/ peers regarding pastoral practices	8E Engages in ministerial self-evaluation on a regular basis
9 Engages in Personal Development	9A Maintains a life of prayer	9B Receives spiritual direction on a regular basis	9C Participates in yearly retreat	9D Nurtures healthy friendships (family/friends)	9E Maintains health (e.g. attends to diet/exercise, physical and mental health)

F	G	H	I	J	K
1F e sick	1G Celebrates the Order of Christian Funerals (wakes/funerals/burials)	1H Leads devotional practices (e.g. Stations, Rosary)	1I Coordinates liturgical planning	1J Oversees the training of liturgical ministers	
2F tes canonical procedures					
3F inates areas of ition (e.g. youth, children)	3G Catechizes adults, youth, children	3H Responds to questions of faith	3I Communicates message of faith through various media	3J Represents the Church's point of view in the public arena	3K Conducts retreats
4F arish	4G Employs parish staff (hires/fires/evaluates)	4H Supervises maintenance of physical plant (Church, school, grounds)	4I Manages parish staff (supervises/supports)	4J Implements diocesan policies	4K Supervises parish communication
5F lies' homes/ er	5G Mediates parish conflicts				
6F iocesan					
7F s on civic, religious unity boards					
8F es to develop- e profession articles, con- research, interacts ht leaders, presentations)	8G Develops a collaborative leadership style	8H Develops multicultural sensitivity			
9F rains balance and n schedule	9G Takes days off and yearly vacations	9H Manages personal finances (e.g. charitable contributions, plans for retirement . . .)			

The Matrix: Duties and Tasks of a Catholic Priest

serving people primarily in parishes, and also in schools, hospitals, prisons, and other settings, through acts of Christian ministry including celebrating liturgy and sacraments, education, administration and pastoral care.